MW01095022

OUTDOOR CHRONICLES

OUTDOOR CHRONICLES

TRUE TALES OF A LIFETIME OF HUNTING AND FISHING

JERRY HAMZA

FOREWORD BY
JOSEPH B. HEALY

SKYHORSE PUBLISHING

Copyright © 2015 by Jerry Hamza
Foreword copyright © 2015 by Joseph B. Healy

Somewhere Down the Crazy River
Lyrics by Robbie Robertson
Copyright © 1987 by Robbie Robertson
All Rights Reserved. Used by Permission
Reprinted by permission of Robbie Robertson

All rights reserved. No part of this book may be reproduced in any manner without the express written consent of the publisher, except in the case of brief excerpts in critical reviews or articles. All inquiries should be addressed to Skyhorse Publishing, 307 West 36th Street, 11th Floor, New York, NY 10018.

Skyhorse Publishing books may be purchased in bulk at special discounts for sales promotion, corporate gifts, fund-raising, or educational purposes. Special editions can also be created to specifications. For details, contact the Special Sales Department, Skyhorse Publishing, 307 West 36th Street, 11th Floor, New York, NY 10018 or info@skyhorsepublishing.com.

Skyhorse® and Skyhorse Publishing® are registered trademarks of Skyhorse Publishing, Inc.®, a Delaware corporation.

Visit our website at www.skyhorsepublishing.com.

10 9 8 7 6 5 4 3 2 1

Library of Congress Cataloging-in-Publication Data

Names: Hamza, Jerry.
Title: Outdoor chronicles : true tales of a lifetime of hunting and fishing / Jerry Hamza ; foreword by Joe Healy.
Description: New York, NY : Skyhorse Publishing, 2015.
Identifiers: LCCN 2015024675| ISBN 9781634504188 (hardcover : alk. paper) | ISBN 9781510701427 (ebook)
Subjects: LCSH: Fishing--Anecdotes. | Hunting--Anecdotes. | Hamza, Jerry. | Outdoor life--Anecdotes.
Classification: LCC SH441 .H26 2015 | DDC 639.2--dc23 LC record available at http://lccn.loc.gov/2015024675

Cover design by Richard Rossiter
Cover photo: Thinkstock

Printed in the United States of America

To my Dad
Through it all, we fished.

Contents

Foreword

As I pass deeper into middle age and approach my fifties, I find myself getting more sentimental than I was in my roaring, invincible youth. I often think fondly (yes, sentimentally) of my preteen years in the Adirondack Mountains region and my teens growing up on the shores of Oneida Lake, outside of Syracuse, New York. That's in the heart of New York State, quite distant from New York City, culturally. Syracuse is middle America, as is about 75 percent of New York State. You may have heard the term Upstate New York, which geographically is the region from Westchester County north to the Empire State's capital city of Albany; however, Central New York is most of what's slightly north and west of there. Buffalo is Western New York, and so is Rochester—at least a little bit. However, I think of Rochester (where my mother was born) predominantly as Central New York. And that belief was confirmed to me when I got to know the writer Jerry Hamza.

This guy Hamza grew up in the Rochester, New York, area and writes about fishing and hunting in the Lake Ontario region of Central and Western New York, and also about his years at Hardwick College near the Catskill Mountains and the famous trout streams there. These are areas I know well, through family connections and life experience. When Jerry writes about fishing for Great Lakes steelhead, I get sentimental because I remember all the times I've done it. Jerry also makes those experiences palpable and real—which shows his value as a writer and storyteller. In a strange coincidence, as an adult I also lived in Coastal Maine and enjoyed visiting Grand Lake Stream in Down East, Maine. Turns out, Jerry has a house there and writes about GLS in this book, too. Weird, huh? Or fate that I got to know this guy Hamza.

Even if you didn't grow up in Central New York or fish Lake Ontario or the Catskills or Grand Lake Stream, Maine, there is much in these pages to keep you entertained.

Speaking of which—I also learned that Entertainment (capital-letter emphasis intended) was Jerry's business for decades as part of the management for the comic George Carlin. That experience opened doors of travel to Jerry, during which he carried fly tackle or a shotgun. He offers stories from those trips, too.

Rollicking fun, adventure, success or not so much, and most of all good thinking characterize these stories. They are the first installment of chronicles from a full outdoor life. Dive in and savor the leisure-time reading. And if you're like me, you'll be waiting eagerly for the next book and the next adventures shared by this guy Hamza.

Joe Healy
Former Associate Publisher
Fly Rod & Reel
Waterford, Vermont
April 2015

Introduction

I spent some time recently in an introspective mood examining what I have become. Like many people, I see life as a process. After around fifty years, I have become a storyteller. Really, it's not a recent happening. In fact, I have been telling stories all my life. The informal sharing of yarns and years of experience has happened for quite a while. It's easy to tell your children how you met the president or the time you shot the eye out of a partridge at hunting camp. In many families, the tales that get passed down from one generation to the next become the colorful oral history of that certain clan.

My transformation from casual fabulist to serious chronicler has to do with a kind of calling. In the past, this same calling led some to decide to become minstrels. In today's world, there are serious challenges to becoming a minstrel—more than finding a costume that fits, even. The best storytellers, such as Mark Twain and Ernest Hemingway, spin their tales in ways that leave you wanting more. They embed subtle anecdotal morals in their stories that sneak up on you and make you think as well as smile. This is the high watermark for which I aim.

It is my pleasure to pass along some of my stories about the human condition set against an outdoor backdrop. In today's world, where it is tempting to live in a virtual world where the electronic environment can isolate us almost completely, I try to refresh the idea that the natural world is beautiful, challenging, rewarding, and real.

It is my hope that you will laugh frequently and think occasionally and lose track of time as you read these stories. That my stories will incite and invite you to recall some of your own. That you will want to make some new ones. That the best revenge is living well, always.

Warmest regards,
Jerry Hamza
Pittsford, New York
Spring 2015

Chapter 1:
Prose to Poetry

"Music, when combined with a pleasurable idea, is poetry; music without the idea is simply music; the idea, without the music, is prose, from its very definitiveness."
—*Edgar Allan Poe*

Bill and I had gone back further than each would like to admit. I really had to sit down and think about where our acquaintance began. It was in the mid-1980s. He had a fishing lodge in northern Ontario. It was a great place to catch giant northern pike on a fly rod and then pick up a few walleyes for shore lunch every day. I loved Bill's place. I would go a couple times a year. It was solitude and isolation.

Bill had a couple of De Havilland floatplanes—usually an Otter and a Beaver. Over the years fishing with Bill, first at his lodge and later at his outpost camp, we would fly in. There was no other way. He always felt that roads to lakes killed the fishing. It is hard to argue with the logic. I was always fascinated by the stories he told about scouting out locations for new outpost camps. It was as simple as flying and landing on unnamed lake after unnamed lake and fishing off the plane's pontoons.

As we would fly to his place, you could see hundreds of lakes in all directions. Most were unnamed. I would ask Bill, "Did you fish there? Did you fish there?"

The answer would be: No, he only fished a very few of the lakes. His search included a set of criteria that ruled out most bodies of water. He was always looking for lakes as locations for outpost camps. This ultimately meant building the camp on "crown land" (this is how Canadians refer to government-controlled land, what U.S. folk call national- or state-park land). Building an outpost on crown land has many regulations. It narrowed Bill's field of interest down to the areas he could use. I, on the other hand, had to deal with the thought of all this water and the possibility that most of it had never seen a fisherman. I felt like a bum looking at a plate of cream puffs through a pastry store window. Years into our affiliation, I finally wore him down. He agreed to keep an eye out for a place. He would find that pristine spot and outfit me for a week. He gave me his word.

One day, the phone rang and Bill was on the line. The odd part was this was November. He asked if I was serious about an outfitted wilderness trip. I told him I was. He let me know these kinds of things could run into money. Everything runs into money, I said. It is the limiting factor of life. Age is the other. If you aren't running out of one you're running out of the other. If you're running out of both, you're fucked.

I asked him how much. He asked me: "How long are you looking to go for?" I told him a week. Bill said, "I probably could get you in there for four or five U.S."

"Where and four or five what?" I answered.

"Somewhere no one has ever fished before. You know all you have to do is show up, eh. The tent and everything will be there for you. That's grand. Come on."

There was a long pause. He knew why. I'm sure the guy in the house next door could hear the wheels in my head turning. It was the chance of a lifetime. An opportunity I had always wanted. How do you put a price on that? Well, Bill just did and it was a steep one, in my world anyway. I told him to give me a few days to figure it out. Reality has screwed up many fine fantasies. How did that saying go? You never see a U-Haul behind a hearse? Of course, no one enjoys financial discord. I sat down and penciled it out. Sacrifices could be made. I figured I could do it for four thousand dollars. A voice in my head said that I should try to chew him down. The smarter voice said that maybe I don't want the guy who was going to outfit me in the middle of nowhere cutting corners to find a profit margin. My motto in recent times has been to err on the side of caution. I told I would do it for four thousand but it would have to be comfortable. This was a lot of money to me. Everything is relative. I would make personal sacrifices to go.

I think it helps in our psyche if things that are important are acquired through struggle and sacrifice. It is the human spirit that enjoys the triumph on the other side of the struggle. For four grand, I hoped so.

So I called Bill back and I was glad to get past the money thing. It is always sort of uncomfortable for me. Over time, I have made friends with some of the people I pay to fish with. I know it's how they feed their families. You have to be so careful. Money has ruined more friendships than sex.

Bill and I moved on to the fishing. He told me he found a great fly-fishing place, maybe. Bill's stock in trade is not fly fishing. It is walleyes. Over the years, he has picked up a couple of us "floaters"—types who go back and forth between fishing styles. I am not sure how endearing a term that is but I am okay with it. I am pretty sure it might be in reference to the flies we float. At least I hope so.

Bill told me he found this gravel bluff overlooking about three miles of a nameless stream between two nameless lakes. That he had landed his plane on one of the lakes last September and caught some nice brook trout at the mouth of the stream. It was connected to the Albany River system so it could be very good. The stream appeared to have a nice gravel bottom and would be good wading, he said. We talked about dates and came up with the first week in August. That far north, it would be like September in the States. I could already feel my fingertips starting to tingle. Sentience is wonderful.

There would be plenty of time to plan. Months to figure out everything. The biggest question would be to go with someone or not. Spending a week with someone in the wilderness is something you really have to pray over. It is not like going to Las Vegas with some friends. When it gets to wearing thin, you can't feign fatigue and skulk up to your room. This is brutal tied-at-the-hip/no-way-out cohabitation for a week. I did a tent-camp hunting trip in Wyoming once. There were three of us. We got caught in the snow storm from hell. We spent ten hard days. In the end there was no hunting and only hard feelings. Years later no one talks still. It was just too much forced time with the wrong blend of guys. I learned then that you really have to be careful; it didn't come to knives at throats but maternal sexuality did come into question.

So that meant going alone. If things went bad, then I would be a victim of my own hand. The biggest concern about doing the trip alone would be safety.

In contemplating safety, you really are dealing with prevention and limitations. To know where the line is and to stay well on the safe side of it. One of the precepts is to check all your equipment. Anything that is worn or the least bit questionable has to be replaced.

Bill and I, over the months, went over the camp outfit several times. In the end I was confident that we had the major points down. The minor points were mine alone. The major points spoke to safety and survival; the minor points were about style and comfort. What good is it if you live through a trip that you suffered through because you didn't sweat the details? If you can say anything about the brutal winters of Upstate New York (where I live), it's that they give you the time to sweat the details.

I knew I would have to rent a satellite phone. Some people embrace technology and this would be fun for them. I am not one of those people. I was pissed when I had to get my first cell phone. I became more pissed when it died and I purchased a Blackberry. When it died my daughter talked me into a smartphone. I am happy to announce that a deer slug propelled down the barrel of a Browning 12-gauge rendered that son of a bitch harmless. I know it was a meaningless act of defiance. In fact, I went out the next day and replaced it. But it was therapeutic and made programming the new phone bearable. On each birthday or Christmas someone feels they need to buy me a Kindle or some likeness of one. They see my beautiful library of leather-bound books and think it a folly. Every year I re-gift them. I just like the way a book feels in my hand. I have a 1983 Honda Civic station wagon that I love. I love her because, besides reminding me of all the road trips of my youth clad in tie-dye, she cannot talk to me. I still pull-start my outboard motor, percolate coffee, and brush my teeth by hand. My solution to the satellite phone situation was to hand it off to my secretary and ask her to make sure it worked.

As I was pondering the minor points of the trip, I knew I'd have to deal with downtime. What I mean is, the time between fishing and running from bears. I could hit poor weather and the evenings needed some filling. Over the years I have become somewhat of a single-malt Scotch aficionado. The truth is sometimes a glass of fine Scotch and a good cigar are pleasures in life. I often forgo the cigar these days for health concerns. I will pack one fine Cuban.

Hey, this will be Canada; they are legal there. I like the twenty-five-year-old Glenlivet but the price tag is too steep. I know it is worth it. I buy one bottle around the holidays and share small glasses with my favorite people. Glenlivet makes a beautiful eighteen-year-old and that would do. I would pack about ten pounds of books. The problem with floatplanes is weight. You have a limit and that is it. If you have ever flown into the woods you have seen that look on the pilot's face as he is figuring out payload in his head. Some outfits have scales at the docks. So you pack according to weight. The nice thing about this trip is that Bill will have had the camp all set before I get there. The tent, cot, table, food, and safe box for the food. Even so, reaching the one-hundred-pound limit for personal equipment can go quick.

The last item I was toying with packing was part of the technology I usually dislike. There are always exceptions. I had purchased an iPod a few years earlier. Recently I had really got into finding my music on the Internet. I was always counterculture. Lately my music was showing up and I could download it. Things like Glen Campbell and the Stone Temple Pilots playing Galveston. Music is an important part of my life. Is it as important as fly fishing or hunting? I can't answer. I need it all. I spent a large portion of my life in the entertainment industry. Actually, we were a family who had deep roots in it. My grandfather and father spent many years promoting country music. Each had a hand in the development of the CMA. As a boy I remember wiping off Loretta Lynn's lipstick from my cheek. Conway Twitty messing up my hair. I remember helping Marty Robbins get his guitar set up at an old theatre in Newark. He would be constantly licking something to soothe his throat. He would leave us soon after. I remember George Jones saying goodbye to my grandfather all choked up. He knew it would be the last time they would work together. Music meant a lot to me and this little iPod device made it reasonable to carry a lot in a very small space. I had been contemplating fishing this trip with it. I kept asking myself if Izaak Walton would fish with an iPod. Then I thought of one of his lines: "Lord, what music hast thou provided for Thy saints in heaven, when Thou affordest bad men such music on Earth!"

I decided I was going to do it. I was also going to bring a docking station and fill the wilderness air with new sounds. There are some who would consider breaking the peace and tranquility of the wilderness with a hot version of Iggy Pop's "The Passenger" a sin. That's okay—as I have established early on, I am indeed a sinner. If we are going to qualify them, with the worst being at the top of the list, this would surely be near the bottom. Right next to paying Suzy Orbacker twenty-five cents to see her underwear in the second grade. She promptly displayed them by opening the brown paper bag she had them in and took my quarter. The gods would forgive me. The bigger problem would be how to keep these things powered. Like most of life's logistical problems it was solved by throwing money at it. Bill would fly in a small generator when he set up camp. Portable electricity is another technology I do not mind.

When we endeavor to undertake a fishing trip, or any trip, there are stages. The first stage is the fanciful stage where it has to appeal. Then comes the reality stage. Can it be done? It is like a decision tree. If it can be done then you have to plan. After planning is the waiting stage. When you are young, the waiting stage is hard. As you age it just lines up with the chronology of life. Then comes the packing stage. This usually takes place late in the waiting stage. Of course, if you have OCD like I do, it can already have taken place several times throughout the waiting stage. Then there is the travel stage. If you do it right, the travel stage can be as good as the main trip. At least a fine hors d'oeuvres to the meal.

The place I had to get to for the floatplane was Geraldton, Ontario. The problem was I was not sure what the hell that is anymore. Literally. Some time in 2001, the Progressive Conservative government of Ontario combined the townships of Beardmore and Nakina, the towns of Geraldton and Longlac with large unincorporated surrounding land districts, and called it Greenstone. You have to figure when the government coops communities someone is going to get screwed. The place I had to get to was the town formerly known as Geraldton. Call it what you will but it sits at 50.0000N, 86.7333W. The good part is it's located just off the Trans-Canadian Highway in the north of the Superior region. This is one of my favorite road trips. If I drove like a maniac infused with Tim's black I could get there in thirty hours. Tim's is Tim Horton's (a chain of excellent coffee franchises), a Canadian cultural fixture. You can't swing a dead cat there without hitting a Tim's. The Red Cross stopped accepting blood from Canadians during the workweek because it was 70 percent Tim's. Though I love Tim's coffee, I would be taking my time. I would make the trip in four days on Tim's Creamy Brown.

I like to take the bridge at Niagara Falls. I just like to see the falls. I also like to see the people who come to see the falls. No matter how you look at it, this is a cool place. "Niagara Falls! Slowly I turned! . . ." One of the most popular vaudeville routines ever. Lundy Lane on the Canadian side is so much fun. You can kill a half-a-day here without any difficulty. I like to time it so I can get into North Bay, Canada, late at night and spend the evening there. I love the city. It is where the big corporations stop spending their money and true *Canadiana* begins. Canadiana is like Americana except it still exists. For instance, if you get to the Ice Hut Bar and Grill in Cochrane, Ontario, you will remember it. The entrées are made up by the proprietors and are really good. It is not franchise bullshit food where you get sick if some worker from Guatemala doesn't wash his hands after taking a shit. You get sick if the person *right here* doesn't wash his hands. I know—but it makes a difference to me. The real point is you have regular people believing in a personal dream putting up their money, their imagination, their sweat, and most of their time to make a business. Here, away from the giant commercial chains, they have a chance. I like people and the personal expression they bring to the world. I hate corporations and the sterilization they inject into us. If you had a terminal disease you could always burn down a Walmart to get square with the house. Besides, the Ice Hut Bar and Grill sells a deep-fried, artery-hardening Mars bar that just kills.

All along Route 11 small businesses create a blend of culture and flavor that is distinctly Canadiana. I always try to take as much extra money as I can. I fill up my car with as much useless shit as I can. I wrap it up and give it to people at Christmas. You can tell where you stand in my world by what you get from me at Christmas. If you get that coin purse made from the bear's scrotum with the Canadian maple leaf stamped on it, you should work on being a little nicer to me in the coming year.

Finally I made it to Bill's place. I was glad to see him. Bill is a good guy. He has that low-key Canadian way. Most of his sentences are finished with "eh" and I just love that too. To top it off he has a big goofy grin. It doesn't matter how pissed you are at him, once he smiles, it's over. "Hey Bill I got you this hand-carved duck," I tell him as I lighten my load by one item. He likes it and places it on his desk so as to cover a pile of paperwork. I think that helps him like it even more. We chat for a while to catch up. He tells me he wants to get me to camp that afternoon. That some rain may come tomorrow. Weather in the north is what you can see. Past that, there is no real certainty. They sell a thing called the weather rock up there. It is a half joke. You have probably seen the likes of it. If the rock is wet, the weather is rainy; if the rock has snow on it, it is snowy; and so on. Bill told me he made a flagpole out of a jack pine. He gave me two flags, one green and one orange. He would fly over every day. If the green flag was flying, he would keep going. He had that big Bill grin on his face when he told me he wanted to show me something. I smiled too. I had an idea about what, but was not sure exactly. I followed him to the dock. I was right. There she was: Bill's new Otter. To the boys in the North Country and Alaska, an Otter is synonymous with a '57 Chevy. They don't make them anymore, guys build the hell out of them, and other guys notice them. This one was a honey. The thing is these are legendary planes and they were built in Canada. They were so important to opening up the Arctic almost globally. So for a Canadian boy it is part of the dream. Bill's new cream puff was a DHC-3 Vazar turbine Otter. It was white with butterscotch stripes and a black streak down the middle. For those of you who don't know planes, just think of a '57 Bel Air built to the hilt. Buffed to a high gloss. The only thing missing was a hot babe adjusting her makeup in the reflection.

"Hey this is so sweet. Throw me the keys!"

"Yeah, right," Bill said.

Bill had a Beaver too. They are both made by De Havilland. The Beaver is smaller than the Otter. It would be far more economical to fly me in the Beaver but I noticed Bill had them loading up the Otter. I love times like this best. When something unpredictable and fun happens in the story. You have to keep watching so you know when you are having the time of your life. I smiled at him. "You figure we need the Otter?"

"Yeah. You know, it doesn't matter how many times I tell you to pack light, eh? Just to show you what a good guy I am . . . no extra charge," he said while flashing his big smile.

"Okay. I suppose we're gonna take the long way, too," I said and smiled back.

"Yup . . . no extra charge."

Not long after he said that he was in the flyer's seat. I got in next to him. The instrumentation was all redone as well. He was so proud and I was impressed. I knew he would let me fly her for a bit when we got up. He put her nose into the wind and lifted off the water like a dream. You could feel the pride float off Bill. I had known Bill long enough to know that this was indeed one of his dreams. I was happy for my friend. I began to look at him in a new light. Dreams are important in life. Dream placement is probably more important. A dream has to be hard enough that the outcome is never sure but not so hard that it can never be. This dream opened the door to the next dream. This plane, as beautiful as she was, could haul around four thousand pounds. That can open a lot of doors in the north.

We ran up to the Albany River. Bill wanted to show me how this water connected to the water along which I would be camping. The Albany River system flows northeast from Lake St. Joseph in northwest Ontario and empties into James Bay. It has many offshoots and has remained primarily wild in its history. The worst exploitation was as a canoe route for furriers in the 1700s. There are several fishing lodges and outfitters that use the system but in the overall picture it amounts to very little pressure. Where Bill had set up was far from anything. He told me the lakes and the stream connecting them were unnamed on all his maps. That if it was fished before, it wasn't in the lifetime of the fish currently living here. He also warned me that just because it was pristine didn't mean fish would rush to impale themselves upon my hook. That I could have bad days here too. I knew all this. I was here for the chance at something special. There was more to all of this than just catching fish. To spend a week in virgin wilderness is something rare. To spend a week isolated and alone is uncommon. Most boys at some point in their lives have wondered about it to the point of fancy—the life of a mountain man. I would not come close to that experience because I was outfitted but I think I could at least feel the nuance. As the Otter landed on the lake, I was wondering if I could stand myself for a week.

Bill circled the lake and dropped our altitude. The pontoons touched the water and the weight of the plane slowly lowered until she was floating. We taxied around until Bill jumped out and tied her to a bush. (Well, that's what you tie planes to in the wilderness.) We unloaded my gear and carried it to the camp, which was located about a quarter mile from the lake. It stood on a bluff overlooking the stream. This stream was a good thirty or forty yards across. In some places it would be called it a river. The bluff stood about a hundred feet high and you could tell at one time the stream flowed this way. It was a good spot for a camp and with a little breeze could provide some relief from the bugs. Bill and crew had done a nice job with the camp. There was a spacious tent with a cot and a lantern. Off to one side of the tent was a tarp and under it was a table and a chair, the generator, a Coleman gas stove, a rack with cooking utensils, eating utensils, and more lanterns. Bill showed me the strongbox filled with provisions. It was a good fifty feet from camp and was padlocked. He gave me the key and smiled. "Don't lose this, eh?"

He was still smiling as we went down to the stream. There in front of a promising-looking pool was a homemade sign. It read "Jerry's Beat." I smiled too. In my mind I was hoping this wasn't putting off the fishing gods. Fishermen are a superstitious bunch. I have a friend who won't get into a boat with tartar sauce present. Another guy threw a full-fledged veins-popping-in-his-forehead rage because the guide had the audacity to have a banana in the boat. I think the only people more superstitious could be hunters. Maybe baseball players. Anyway, the sign made me a little nervous. I followed Bill back to the plane to see him off. He reminded me about the green and orange flags. Then he threw a package at me.

"What's this?" I said.

"Walleye fillets! I'll see you in a week. Have fun."

He smiled, climbed into the plane, and had her nose into the wind. He took his beautiful Otter once around the lake and tipped his wing at me. I liked Bill. The walleye fillets would be a great dinner. By the time I got unpacked and had all my stuff situated, it was dinnertime. I decided I would have a walleye shore lunch. A true treat. Simply dredge the fillets in flour with salt and pepper. Then slice some potatoes and onions thin. It reminded me of the days when I first started fishing. Particularly in this part of the world. Walleye was the game and there was a morning session and an evening session. There was a guide with wonderful cedar-strip boats. The whole day was accentuated by the shore lunch. The guide would fillet the morning catch. Prepare the potatoes and onions. There was always a can of Spam. It was insurance against getting skunked. The shore-lunch spots had a fireplace made of granite rocks arranged in a ring so as the size allowed for the big long-handled frying pan to rest nicely over the fire. The guide would gather up dry deadwood, start the fire, and put the pan over it. Then, unbelievable in today's world, he'd put a couple pounds of pure lard into the pan. I cannot tell you how much time of my mortality melted in the frying pan with all that lard. I can tell you it was a culinary delight. I would try to recreate that with a slightly more cardiac-friendly olive oil. It was a fine dinner. I was careful to clean everything up at the stream. There were plenty of black bears here. It would be great if we just kept a respectful distance.

After dinner, I took the time to make ready all the things I would need for the following day. I started with my fishing vest. It has become an old friend. It is the old-school kind with lots of pockets and zippers and snaps. The part I like best is no Velcro. It was a good vest when I purchased it, still is. After all these years the only thing wrong is that it has faded some, but so have I. I always change the pocket contents for the immediate trip. I loaded the leader I wanted, the bug dope, tippets, bug spray, sunscreen, hard candy, satellite phone, squeezed on hemostats, the Cohiba, a lighter, and my flask. I pulled out my old pair of Simms neoprene waders. They have been patched so many times, they have become an old friend. I know I am never going to be on the cover of any catalog. I like that. Catalog covers are so overrated. I string up a nice Winston 4-weight, quick and tough. I put together a fly box with a lot of terrestrial patterns.

I have even added a few small mousies—flies tied to imitate small mice. I would love to catch a brook trout on a mouse pattern. I have always wanted to. As I get older I find that how I catch fish rivals the act of catching fish. I love catching them on the surface. If you told me that I could catch ten fish under the surface for every one I caught on top, I would probably fish that much harder with a dry fly.

The morning came and I rose with the sun. Sleeping comes with such struggle on the eve of a new outdoor experience. Often, morning is an act of mercy. So much more this morning.

I began to dress. It's funny how you notice certain things as you get older. Sometimes you really have to concentrate on the act of buttoning. Your brain tells your fingers what to do. It's just that your fingers are not so ready to get the message. I am not sure where the disconnect is. It is just not that automatic. I sometimes have the same issues on the stream tying on a fly. If you are younger and cannot relate, don't worry too much. It will come to you. The other thing that comes with maturity is the idea that steel-cut oats make a fine breakfast. I now believe that and enjoyed them that morning. Sitting at the table liking the way the warm oatmeal was feeling inside me along with the fresh wilderness air was my iPod. I put it there. I was having a crisis of conscience of sorts. I knew I had decided I was going to fish with it. It was just getting to do it for the first time that was difficult. I know it shouldn't be a big deal but for me it was. I had always held the sounds and cadences of the natural world as special. In that reverence I had kept my life very clean and separate. I know to some it sounds like a bit too much. If you throw in a good measure of OCD then it might make more sense.

I put the iPod in the docking station while I ate breakfast. All of a sudden Steely Dan's "Deacon Blues" was echoing across the flat bed and stream area beneath the camp. I am sure for the first time in the history of the ages a saxophone solo wafted across this little valley. Very cool. I enjoyed the music all through breakfast. I decided I would wait to fish with the music. I made sense of it with the logic that the first day needed my undivided attention to figure out this new place. The reality was I was biding my time. Like deciding to have sex with someone for the first time. You can rationalize it but it is very different when the moment comes. It is an emotional commitment. I needed to get going. It was a blue sky, high-pressure-system day. I wondered how that would go. The best way to find out would be to fish. So I did.

As I got into the stream, I realized how well Bill picked this place. There were so many places where the bank had a gradual grade into the water. The gravel bed itself was a dream to wade. It consisted of large gravel anywhere from the size of a cherry to a tangerine. They were bits of granite worn smooth over the millennium. Each rock with its own color. Some red, some white, some black, and some an amalgamation. It had the effect of an impressionistic painting. Claude Monet could have added each with little dabs of his brush. I realized that indeed this was no accident. Quite thoughtful for a guy who didn't fly fish. It meant he took the time to figure out what I would need. It reminded me that good friendship involves work and selflessness. Then I thought about the hand-carved duck I put on Bill's desk. That's how it is.

One of the things that became obvious was, with the blue sky, fish were spooky. In a place where man never impacted the predator base, a day like this was high alert for a trout interested in survival. It turned out that the hardest part was the approach. If I could get a fly on the water without spooking the fish, something would eat it. Again we tend to think in terms of our manicured places. Here things were as they grew. Some casts were likely to produce suckers and others brook trout. In the end, both took flies off the surface, fought hard, and provided good sport. It was such a terrible prejudice I had at first. I was pissed when the first sucker came onto the gravel bank. Fly-fishing snobbery. You really have to think it through. There is a place that I fish in the spring. You can catch giant rock bass on a fly rod. They come there to spawn. It is not a problem to catch a dozen of them over a pound and approaching two pounds in a couple hours. They are an angry fish right down to their fiery red eyes. I can get pretty smug about it because I figure it's all mine. Who else is going to want to catch rock bass on a bamboo fly rod regardless of how big? When I ask someone if they would like to come fish with me, I usually get an eye roll. It must be fly fishing's version of slumming it. I had to adopt that train of thought about the suckers. I enjoyed each fish on the merit of the fight they gave me.

Even with the attitude adjustment, it is hard to deny that brook trout are special. Early August in this part of the world was fall. The brook trout in my hands was telling that tale so clear. He had a kype in his jaw and his flanks were a bright reddish-orange. It was hard to compute an equal in your head when you are looking at this. This is clearly why I had gone to so much trouble. There was no equal. The suckers were the ugly sisters. I just had to be respectful. I would have to figure out how to pattern the brookies so much better.

The second morning was similar to the first. A soaring high-pressure system was still in place but conditions would be changing. I could see the mares' tails in the sky. Mares' tails are a kind of cloud. A cirrus uncinus cloud. The Latin translation means "curly hooks" but they do resemble mares' tails. They are a high wispy cloud that is generally seen when a warm or occluded front is approaching. When they show up the weather will change within twenty-four hours. Fishermen have all sorts of theories when it comes to weather and its effects on the fishing. Science has weighed in. Still I cannot find a clear representation of what is true. The only real truth I can tell you is that fishing in a boat with a graphite rod in your hand during a thunderstorm is not smart. I have not done it. It is not smart. Other than that, most of the information is conflicting. Some guys like a dark overcast day, with or without precipitation. West wind, north, south—most dislike an east wind. I have done well in almost everything. In my own meandering experience I have found a falling barometer good. What does that mean? Nothing more than I prefer it. That I will fish tomorrow's falling barometer with more confidence. Sometimes it is our attitude that contributes more than anything to success. Why should fishing be different than other factors in life? Beyond the thought of the falling barometer I thought the steel-cut oats for breakfast would do well with a handful of wild blueberries.

I was beginning to pattern the fishing here and it was good. Most of the trout were ten to twelve inches. Every now and then a bigger fish of twenty to twenty-two inches would take the fly. I was fishing a size 12 Jay Dave's Hopper. It was fishing very well and for the most part seemed to be preferred by the brook trout over the suckers. I was working my way downstream to a meadow filled with wild blueberry bushes. I had a small Tupperware in my vest for the express purpose of scoring some fresh fruit for the next day's oatmeal.

Fishing the hopper along the far bank just below some overhanging dry grasses made my mind drift to some of Nick Adams' stories. Some say that "Big Two-Hearted River" is devoid of a plot. I just cannot agree with that. When Nick finally speaks, "*Go on, hopper . . . Fly away somewhere,*" he is summing up his desire and the American desire to just get away. It is in us and at our core. During the Great Depression, men would ride the rails. It is so well portrayed in many of Jimmie Rodgers' works. Then we would run away and join the circus. In my time it was attractions such as following the Grateful Dead. More recently standing in an unnamed stream disconnected from the tensions of the hard society we created. It is good for the soul.

I fished to the blueberry meadow. It had a wonderful smell. The cool nights were fixing the fructose in the berries. You could smell the sweetness in the vast area of bushes. At first I was eating the berries. Wild blueberries are very similar to their domestic cousins in everything except they tend to be smaller and a bit sweeter. I was truly enjoying the experience to the point at which I was oblivious to almost everything around me. My container was almost full when I heard the heavy snap of a large stick breaking. My head shot up in the direction of the noise. Perhaps a hundred feet away was a black bear boar doing what I was doing too. It was a real primal moment. The hair on the back of your neck stands and your flight or fight instinct starts to percolate. Your mind searches its database for the appropriate ideas. Then you have to decide which ones are the right ones. Intelligence is really two things: the ability to remember things you have learned correctly and the judgment on when to use what you recall. Evolution is when something eats the individual who chooses wrong. I remember reading that running in this instance would be the wrong move. I also know from fishing in Alaska that it would be a good idea to let the bear know I was there. Gathering up all my bear knowledge and applying it led me to standing up and waving my arms and shouting, "Hey you blueberry-eating son of a bitch, I am here with you!"

At that point the bear stood up. I am not sure if he wanted to take a better look at me or took offense at being called a blueberry-eating son of a bitch. I stood tall and held my arms up and out to my sides to look as big as I could. I imagine being a bit over six feet tall and 260 pounds didn't hurt but at the moment I felt very small. I kept talking loudly at him and he kept standing and trying to get my wind. Eventually he must have as he lowered and ran the other way. It may have been the first time he ever scented man. It was the slowest time ever moved for me. I am not sure if I handled it right. It probably didn't hurt that there were plenty of berries for all.

The bear scare aside, the rest of the afternoon was a fine one. After a while I was even able to put the encounter in perspective and like it. As I returned to camp, I decided I would make pasta for dinner and put the iPod in the dock again. That evening after dinner I was reading and listening. I had the music cranked way up and "The Ballad of Peter Pumpkinhead" by XTC played loud and clear. You could hear the harmonies echo for a long way. In the night it inspired the accompaniment. Wolves began to howl along with the music. I laughed out loud. I put down my book and listened. It was not hard to feel that they were singing along with the music. When Kate Bush's "Wuthering Heights" began to play, it seemed that you could hear the joy in their howls. For them it was an alien encounter. For me it was just a bit of magic in the night. One of those moments that you cannot make happen but just have to live and be thankful you get to have.

The next morning proved that the mares' tails told their fortune yet again. The morning was gray with a damp mist in the air. The oatmeal would feel extra good, both for the fresh blueberries and the way it would stick to my ribs. With the music still fresh in my head from the night before, I decided today would be the day I broke with my long tradition. I removed the iPod from the dock and positioned it in a top pocket in my vest. I brought out the ear buds and zipped the pocket as close to shut as I could. Sleeping outdoors in damp weather gets me a little stiff these days. I did a bit of stretching. I decided to gather firewood before I went fishing. I knew I would have a chill at the end of the day. A down sleeping bag will eventually warm you but it just cannot compete with a roaring campfire. Few things in life can compete with a well-placed campfire.

As I approached my stream—it had no name and therefore had become mine—I noticed a hatch. I thought I recognized the big meaty bugs but I had to catch one to be sure. They were the legends of the flies. It was a Green Drake hatch! If fly fishing has a holy grail, this is it. The fish seem to relish these bugs. Their size makes them a protein jackpot, but there is something more. They must be delicious. I have not eaten one but the way fish prefer them is really telling. I have always wanted to ask those folks who eat bugs how Green Drakes stack up. The problem is I just never spend any time around bug-eaters. We just don't travel in the same circles.

I tied on a big delicious-looking Green Drake pattern, put the buds in my ears, and turned on the music. Joseph Arthur's "In the Sun" was the first song I fished to. During the refrain of "May God's love be with you" a nice, fat brook trout smacked my fly. Next came "We're Not Kids Anymore," a live version by Loretta Lynn and Ernest Tubb. The music on my iPod is eclectic and reflects me well. I am guessing everyone's is like that. At some point someone will do a study in which your psychological profile can be arrived at from a study of your iPod.

After about an hour, something wonderful began to happen. Things began to sync up. The marvelous hatch, the music, and my casting. I am standing there in the middle of nowhere casting in rhythm to the music. Shaking my head and my ass, putting down beautiful cast after cast. Feeling the rhythm of the music align with the rhythm of the day. There are those who say if you start Pink Floyd's "Dark Side of the Moon" at just the right time with the *Wizard of Oz* it syncs up perfectly and is pretty wild to watch. They call it "Dark Side of the Rainbow." In 2000, the cable channel Turner Classic Movies aired "*Oz* with the Dark Side album" as an alternative soundtrack.

In similar fashion, I am aligning with the music and the nature of it all. Miles Davis is blowing hard in a fine version of "Time After Time" when a giant female brook trout crushes my fly. As his horn is blowing to a crescendo I am looking at my reel spinning into its backing. The sound of line coming off my reel sounds like Miles Davis hitting a high note. I smile as I finally turn the fish. As I beach the beauty I notice she is fat with spawn and must be an easy three pounds. John Prine and Iris DeMent are singing "In Spite of Ourselves" in my ear at this point. I notice time has slipped by. I have fished my way down to where my stream pours into my lake. The Drake hatch is waning a bit and I feel like this might be the time and place to tie on the mouse fly.

I take the music out of my ears for a minute. I need to just assess for a bit. I tie on the light-tan mouse. I am on the north side of the stream. There is a bit of a drop off as the stream meets the lake. I cannot see the bottom. Experience tells us big fish wait here for food to come to them. I test the knot I've tied, put the music back, and find the rhythm right where I left off. An especially hot version of the Grateful Dead's "Bertha" live comes on. It is a song that can really get me dancing. I was there in the northern Canadian woods shaking my booty for all it was worth. I was free and feeling like it. It is good just to let go at times. Knowing there is no other soul for miles to witness it helps in the process. Sometimes catharsis can be serious business but this was lighthearted and fun. Even when the mouse got smacked I kept dancing. Big brook trout. Heck, he ate a mammal. A different song would come on and the groove would rise and ebb but never quit. Big brook trout were feeling something on the same wavelength. The food was moving and they needed to beef up for the long, hard northern winter. They were in their own groove. What a great day, we had overlapping grooves!

The fishing at that spot was crazy. I had just released another three-pound trout a while earlier. I had lost my first mouse in a tree. It happens. This mouse was getting pretty long in the tooth. It seemed before each cast I had to align the deer-hair body over the hook shank. I had one more mouse but it was bigger. I was a little miffed at myself. I always get that way when I run low or out of the hot fly. These were mice patterns. I packed them on a whim. Who uses mouse flies outside of Alaska? Anyway, here I was with a big mouse. It was late in the day, I had caught plenty of big fish, and I was happy. I was getting philosophical about the day. That usually means times are good. I settled back into the music and the casting. I knew a hit on such a big fly would be remote. I decided to concentrate on the scenery with a nice soundtrack. I started watching an eagle fishing out over the lake as Jose Feliciano sang a moving version of "California Dreaming." My mind began to wonder over some of the places I had fished in the past. I was slipping into that auto-cast mode. Joan Baez sang "Diamonds and Rust." Before the trip I wondered if I could take a week with myself. It was turning out I could; in fact, it let me figure out some things without distraction.

As I listened, one of my favorite songs came on. It is an unlikely collaboration between Lyle Lovett and Al Green, a tune called "Funny How Time Slips Away." It was written by Willie Nelson but this performance is smoking soul. The first time I heard it I was in a store and I stood staring at the speaker slack-jawed. It just plain smokes. I am enjoying it and casting, casting and grooving, and *bam*. In a moment reality snaps in without warning. My rod is pointing straight to the east. Line is churning off the reel. The human brain is an amazing device. It is capable of making thousands of calculations all at once. Mine was doing them all. I was into the backing and the fish was not slowing down. I pulled out the iPod and set it on the ground, tightened the safety belt around my waist, and the one at my chest. What the hell was it? I knew it wasn't a brook trout. It was something that eats brook trout. It was running up the south side of the lake. I was going to have to cross the stream. As I walked into the water I felt the bottom drop away. I stuck my rod arm high and tried to catch the breath the cold water took away. I managed to reach the other bank and the fish had slowed. Not because I did anything but rather he felt he was far away from the initial annoyance. I gained back line and applied pressure again. This went on for the better part of an hour. Finally we met. Tired and finning was the biggest northern pike I had ever seen. It was well over forty inches long. I set my rod next to her and marked her length with a pencil. She was thick across the back. I was guessing she had to approach thirty pounds. Why not? She probably made her living sitting there eating fat, three-pound brook trout. Nothing was going to bother her. She was the apex predator in that water. The Latin name for the northern pike is *Esox lucius,* which can be loosely translated to hungry wolf. She belonged here and I revived her and let her go.

I thought about the hungry wolf. That made me think about how nice it would be to have a fine baked brook trout for supper. I worked my way back to where I left my iPod. I took the long way back and crossed my stream at a much more shallow crossing. I picked up my iPod and restored my setup. I tied on a Green Drake fly pattern and was back in business. It did not take long to catch a fat trout. I decided that would be dinner and that was enough. I sat on a rock and drew out my flask and took a long sip of the Scotch. I then rifled through my pockets until I found the baggie that held the Cohiba and the lighter. There are two types of Cohibas. They both come from the same people. The first can be sold in America but they are made in the Dominican Republic to solve ancient political issues. The cigars taste like they have been made to solve ancient political issues. The second are authentic Cuban products. The official stogies of the head honcho of cigarland, Fidel Castro. They undergo an extra fermentation process with top-quality Cuban leaf and it is heaven. Cuban Cohibas are legal fare in Canada and that is what was in my baggie. So there I was an American of Italian and Lebanese decent in the Canadian wilderness drinking Scottish whisky while smoking a Cuban cigar listening to an iPod made in China. It took roughly three million years of evolution for this day to happen.

I eventually worked my way back to camp. There are good days afield and there are great ones. This day was the latter. Somehow they just come together on you. There were parts of the day I replayed while I made the nice but simple baked-trout dinner. I had one of those astronaut apple-fritter desserts and it was pretty darned good. I had changed my clothes earlier but the chill was still inside me from my unscheduled swim. In my heart I was looking forward to the fire. There is something deep inside us that feels spiritual next to the roar of a fire in the dark night. As the dusk was deepening, there was some clearing, a hint of promise for some moon. I had the iPod in the dock again. I lit the fire. It was easier to take sips of the Scotch. Between the heat of the fire and the whisky, my muscles started to let go. Doc Watson came on the iPod with a soulful rendition of "Summertime." I re-lit the cigar I had saved. One of the books I had taken with me was a collection of Poe. I love to read Poe. Poe had these thoughts about music applied to life. "Music, when combined with a pleasurable idea, is poetry; music without the idea is simply music; the idea, without the music, is prose, from its very definitiveness." In thinking that through for some time, I realized that on this day I was a poet fisherman. I liked that.

The rest of the trip saw heavy rains. It can happen that way. I spent most of the rest of the trip reading in the tent. How much can you write about when nothing happens? Things do often come in balance, of course. In the rain, I could sort out some of what happened. I knew there would be other days to fish with music; they would be whimsical days. I came to the water's edge for solace and I now had the option to fish with music. I liked the added dimension. As I was waiting to hear the drone of the Otter in the distance, I felt the need to fix the sign Bill had placed by the water's edge. It now reads: "Jerry's Beat Goes On."

Chapter 2:
The Outdoorsman

"The sun with all those planets revolving around it and depending upon it, can still ripen a bunch of grapes as if it had nothing else in the universe to do."

—*Galileo*

It is my fiftieth year and I find myself alone. I have no significant other. I am not melancholy about it. In fact, the situation was bought about by my own hand. I looked up at my long-term girlfriend and just didn't love her anymore. It has tragic overtones but really it is common, to be honest, and therefore much less tragic if even at all. I ended it and ended up alone, again. It has been done before. In fifty years there is bound to be some repetition. She was a nice lady. They do happen. My friends would mention, at first, that I should not worry. I was not worried but I must have looked worried because it was a common message. Then there were the offers "to help." My friends always seemed to know someone who might like me. These conversations would stir something old and distant in the cortex of my brain. The Rolodex would start to churn. Some sort of warning sequence would fire and the words "fix up" would pop. Many years ago, I had been fixed up and memories of sneaking out through the back door of a restaurant and changing my phone number became clear. Fuck that.

There are always good intentions among friends and often their efforts must be headed off to maintain the friendship and happiness. I needed to be proactive and find some type of woman, they would say. I was not unhappy but I sensed this issue would not go away. I came up with the strategy of online dating.

I am not exactly the cyber-techno geek type. I was pissed when I had to buy a cell phone and cried when my flip phone died. My daughter talked me into buying an iPhone to replace it. I don't like it.

Turns out I liked online dating even less. I thought it would be easier to control situations. I could punch in movies twice a month, dinner on Thursdays, TV and popcorn every other Tuesday, and some good sex after the dinners and popcorn. A few weeks later and my cyber counterpart would knock on my door all dolled up for dinner and a movie followed by an evening of middle-aged passion.

Truth is I did not even finish my profile. You have to fill out a profile describing who you are. I started out with the usual junk—loving, caring, hardworking, blah blah blah. It gave me pause so I started looking at everyone else's. What a bunch of soulless shit. No wonder they were alone. It did make me think. I took out pen and paper. I started jotting down who I was. Avid outdoorsman. I wrote that. Avid Outdoorsman. I looked at that. I sat and thought about it for a while. I removed my profile and went to bed.

Next morning I woke up and there was that sheet of paper. "Avid Outdoorsman." I thought about it. What a stupid fucking qualifier *avid* is. I crossed it off.

The paper now just read "outdoorsman." I stared at it for some time. I reflected over my years and it was me. In my life, through the women, jobs, children, houses, boats, cars, glasses, illnesses, speeding tickets, and crème brûlées is . . . fishing and hunting.

It was nice to know my life had a theme. I know some people don't care for it these days. I get "Oh you hunt?" or "Fishing? Can't that be cruel?" It depends on my mood. I like to think time has mellowed me some. I try to be nice and say, "I am waiting for your husband to have some extra time to teach me how to drink and screw my secretary . . . then I will switch."

I really like nervous laughter from self-righteous people. If you are an outdoorsperson you just get "it." You understand that it is in your soul and it is a part of you just like your sexuality.

I come from people who fish and there are some who say that is where I get it from. Those same people were not hunters and never had guns. I was not allowed to own a gun until no one but me could decide. On my eighteenth birthday I purchased my first hunting license. Forget that it was April. I try to tell people that it is my instinct, just like the wolf. They give me the evolution crap. I tell them it has only been a few hundred months since grocery stores have been putting meat in pretty styrofoam packages. Most of the time to no avail. I just have to tell them they are the pinnacle of evolution and I am much closer to the cave. Could they please cut me a little slack while I try to catch up evolutionarily?

I like to consider myself in a evolutionary eddy. It absolves me of a lot of mankind's sins. It's like when I had my apple farm and the whole wonderful dinner came off the farm or from produce traded with neighbors. When the Amish moved into the area, it was downright rapture. The Thanksgiving feast was a turkey, venison cutlets (made very Italian with Nana's recipe), apple-and-cornbread stuffing, mashed potatoes, creamed corn, apple pie, rhubarb pie, apple juice, and apple jack. It was easy to get smug and self-righteous. You would think, let those maniacs blow themselves up, who needs civilization? It's all crap. The tractors I was running burned diesel without regard, and the chemicals I was spraying were so much science and technology. The truth is my ass was toast with the rest of the world but my apple farming felt good and I gave sincere thanks. I still do.

I am thankful to be able to live the life of an outdoorsman. Anyone who spends enough time in nature learns to recognize her voice. I have always had a lady in my life. The native people understood this and often refer to Mother Earth. It takes time and desire to hear the cadence of it all. Each season and situation has subtle cues. They used to be much easier to hear. In our modern age all the technology has created its own noise. It often rises to levels so loud that we have a generation on the ground with members who have never heard the whisper of a trout stream or been in a snow-covered forest. It is this movement and symphony of nature that has driven my life. It is the women of the season that really has crowded out the other women in my life over the years.

In my youth, I suffered from the common delusion most young sportsmen have. The idea that you can have it all. You can find a beautiful woman who will hunt and fish with you. A girl who will paddle from the front of the canoe. (Some of us have had the balls to try for "on at the rear of the canoe.") A girl that will filet fish, clean grouse, drag deer, cook venison chili at camp, massage your back, and give you great sex, all before setting the alarm clock so she can get up and make breakfast before she loads up the canoe for the next day's outing.

I remember a local game warden we so affectionately called Bobberhead sneaking up on me having sex in the goldenrod a few yards away from unattended rods. I was pretty embarrassed. He pulled me aside. Looked me in the eye and said, "Don't get used to it." I had no idea what he was talking about. I inquired if I did something wrong he should tell me because I was a good sportsman and upholding the fish-and-game regulations meant something to me. He told me I was in compliance. He told me time would tell. It took time but I got it.

Outdoorsmen are somewhat of an enigma for women. The only chance they have is if their father was one. Things are changing as some fathers are taking their daughters in the field with them. It makes that match of a sportsman with a sportswoman more likely although not quite on the fantasy level. I am guessing the field is level or a bit chivalrous. I watch some of these outdoor shows that feature couples and it is nice.

In my life, the women who have gone afield with me have done so to try and be with me. Most cases it was a selfless gesture. My friend Don's wife Nancy had a good take on it: "He doesn't drink, do drugs, or chase women, I know where he is. I get to see him December, January, and February. I am usually glad when March comes."

Because I'm an outdoorsman, someone once asked me my favorite month. I said October. As I have aged, fly fishing and bowhunting have really become passions. I can also do some bird hunting in that month as well. You add to that fall colors and cool days and it suites me. I love the smell of October. It is sweet and easy to breathe. It is the giving part of the cycle. Nature has worked and cycled. All the outdoors has grasped toward the sun since spring. Her face pining toward the hydrogen fusions exciting photosynthesis. She grabs the sun's rays from the spring till now to peak in harvest. Many harvests. I like to enjoy all of those I can. I pack a small pack. Small cast-iron frying pan. Small coffee pot. Small tin of truffle butter. A couple slices of homemade garlic rosemary bread. A bottle of water. It weighs fifteen pounds. Maybe.

I have this pretty Browning 20-gauge. In my youth, I loved the 12-gauge. It was all about power. Magnums and three-and-a-half-inch shells. Now my shoulder hurts. I value finesse somehow. I also value pretty.

Somewhere along the line I was programmed to not value pretty. It wasn't manly. As if I liked pretty things I was going to burst out of a closet somewhere in pumps and a push-up bra singing show tunes. I really don't have anything against those things but I would look bad. In the big scheme the creator probably erred on the side of caution. My 20-gauge is a pretty gun. It has nice engraving and gold inlay. The stock is prime walnut. It is a light and pleasing gun to hold. The best part is it shoots just like it looks. It is a promise kept.

Early in the morning in October the gun, the pack, and I go into the woods looking for ruffed grouse. For those of you who live in the Northeast I have said enough. For the rest, the ruffed grouse is a fine upland gamebird. It can be hunted over dogs or not. It likes the woods of the Northeast. It looks like a small turkey but much prettier. A bird pretty enough to be shot with my gun. They can flush extremely fast, or not at all. I mean, they have been known to just sit there and think they are fine. Lots of grouse have been shot two feet from a truck door right off a branch or on the ground. It is because they are cursed.

Grouse are delicious and people want to eat them. I have heard some people are hunting them with a bow. Sounds like something to try. They do get even. They have a habit of resting right under the snow. Breaking only at the last minute as you are a foot or two away. Literally scaring the crap out of hunters and ruining undergarments every season. I prefer to shoot them on the wing. Not preaching, just my choice.

It was a classic fall morning. Frost was still on the goldenrod that filled the field in front of the woods I had chosen. It looked like a white lace doily on a dark oak table. The smell filled my head. It is sweet with the start of the leaf drop. There are sugar maples here. For some reason when their leaves first fall and start to decay it is sweet and lovely. I move forward slow. I just need one bird, perhaps two. Without a dog it is a reachable goal for lunch. The problem about hunting stories is unless you are hunting a rabid grizzly and your gun misfires, it is over when the trigger is pulled. The understanding is that it is about everything. As I age I know this and I make sure I take it all in. That sounds corny but I even enjoy buying and grinding special beans for my forest coffee.

Out of the corner of my eye there he is. I don't know how I do that. I just do. It is a sense in me. All of a sudden I just know. It is my natural eye. The instinct that we have been trying to cover up for hundreds of years or more. The primal eye and attitude.

I start to pick the shape out of the surroundings. My ruffed grouse. He is sitting atop a stump. I have him sized up. I know how I will approach him. I have done this before. I want him to flush to my right if I can. It is a good day and the bird accommodates my being left-handed. He is a nice grouse. I harvest a big breast. It will be plenty for lunch. I take some feathers. I don't tie flies. I tried but it didn't work out. I take them for a friend who takes my donations and in return gives me a few flies that will actually catch fish. I take a few of the bigger tail feathers for my cat. She loves them and we have fun playing. It is no accident that I am here with my pack. I have been here before. It is a favorite place. There is a clearing with and old stone foundation of some kind. I like to build my fire near the foundation. There is also an old pear tree and I am hoping to peal a couple with sugar. It is a beautiful fall day. I start my fire, put the pan and butter on. While I am making my coffee I go get my pears. The tree is full. Beautiful green with a crimson blush, they are ripe and ready. I pick two. Out of the corner of my eye, again my primal eye spots a grape vine. It is an old abandoned vine but for some reason it has a few large (by wild standards) grapes. I feel lucky to encounter such a nice bonus. With today's bounty it almost feels greedy. I peel and dice the pears and split the grapes and add sugar and let them sit in a container.

We all have our days. Those days when it goes our way and we enjoy and, if we are smart, appreciate. That was my day. I cooked the breast with some dandelion greens. I never drink coffee except like this; it was very good. I came to my dessert. It was just a moment. The grapes . . . the grapes were so good it made me think: A quote of Galileo's came to mind. It is about how the busy sun has the time to ripen to perfection some grapes, just for me. It made me think about my being an outdoorsman. What that meant. I understood that my affair with nature has made it hard to keep relationships with real women. At this point some authors would break out all kinds of symbolism. How communing with nature was the real relationship. How any other woman would just be a mistress to her. That upon reflection I had found the true love of my life early on and it took until now to realize her and appreciate her. Now in the glow of this epiphany my life is complete. Talk about horse shit.

On some Wednesday night when for whatever reason your body decides to rush a bunch of testosterone (or estrogen, as the case may be) in your system, forget taking nature home to fuck your lights out. I have a different perspective. This being an outdoorsman is a calling. It chose me and I cannot resist. It is usually solitary. It doesn't involve fucking (as good as that always is). It involves eating wild grapes with sugar after shooting a wild grouse. Or catching a brook trout wearing its spawning colors in the fall.

I have to be honest with the people I choose to share my life with. I must obey these callings to my soul but after that I can share the rest with you. By the way, can you come over for dinner Wednesday night?

Chapter 3:
Eastern Steelhead

"What have I become
My sweetest friend
Everyone I know goes away in the end
And you could have it all
My empire of dirt."
—*Trent Reznor, Nine Inch Nails, from the song "Hurt"*

I have some West Coast friends who occasionally ask me to donate money to help in their battle to preserve their steelhead fishery. I give what I can. I understand the genuine distress they feel over the decline of one of the greatest fisheries on the planet. The steelhead trout is a creature whose mythology is well deserved. The most common description is a rainbow trout on steroids. That really doesn't come close to getting there. Genetically, the description is close. To put that in perspective, we share 50 percent of our DNA with a banana, 60 percent with a fruit fly, 75 percent with a mouse, 80 percent with a cow, and more than 98 percent with a chimp. Small amounts make big differences. So much so that the people who are in the middle of these conservation battles want different strains recognized and protected. The fish have evolved differently in each drainage, meaning steelhead have a slightly different character from fishery to fishery. Like sisters from the same parents. Some have asked if I can sum up what makes a steelhead a steelhead? It is simply a rainbow trout that took an anadromous turn. It was this genetic left turn that also required the fish to get tough to hack it in big water. Very tough.

Occasionally, I get invited out to the West Coast and partake in traditional fly fishing for steelhead. There are some places located on British Columbia's Skeena watershed I absolutely adore. Regrettably over the years, I have noticed the decline of steelhead in some of the more traditional rivers. I know the debate rages over causes and cures. I live on the other side of the continent. My ability to help is limited to the twenty dollars I can stick in an envelope. I love the fish but geography can be a great barrier. Sometimes there can be other barriers, as well—the walls we erect in our hearts and minds. These same people who invite me to fish with them and help them ball right up at the mention of Great Lakes steelhead.

The Great Lakes steelhead program has a long and interesting history. In 1876, Michigan began planting Campbell Creek and McCloud River strains from California and fish from the Klamath River in Oregon. Recent creel studies have shown that the Michigan steelie has become wild and evolved into its own animal. The Great Lakes have had steelhead and biologists have managed them for 120 years. In my neck of the woods in New York State, mainly the Washington steelhead were stocked here. Usually six to twelve pounds of bad, bad, bad temper. There are other strains but the only real impact is when they may sneak into your favorite stream. The experts explain that the juvenile fish imprint on the unique odor of the watershed. This is mostly true. I believe any little tributary with a gravel bottom and a similar smell will capture steelhead runs. I more than believe it; I fish it. (The other great characteristic of steelhead is they can be ravenous and eagerly take flies, while Pacific salmon stocked in the Great Lakes won't because they're spawning.)

I do fish the better-known streams in Western New York and the Great Lakes, and the fishing is wonderful. Steelhead fishing usually starts in September with the fish following the salmon (also stocked in the Great Lakes). Our Great Lakes do a fine job of mimicking the great salmon food cycle in the Pacific Northwest. The tributaries of Lake Ontario never cease to amaze me: In August you could swing a cat and see neither fish nor fowl; by early October you could catch three kinds of salmon and three kinds of trout all better than ten pounds on the same day. I have not done that but I have come close. (Atlantic salmon are very rare here.) Though the major tributaries are wonderful and provide room to cast, my favorite water will not appear in any brochure or on a web site. It won't appear in this story, either. It really cannot. It is a small creek that, for some reason, steelhead like.

At its widest spot my creek is perhaps twenty yards; most of it is much smaller. There are really four pools, which I have poetically named Pool One, Two, Three, and Five. Four was a mistake and had to be dropped. It seems my creek, at one point, must have smelled like one of the stocked tributaries. Some steelhead found there way there. Some still do but a fair number are now born there. The New York State Department of Conservation clips a fin of the fish it stocks. About half the fish I catch are without clipped fins. You can tell a bit about the fish from the clip—sometimes even the hatchery it came from. Those without a clipped fin are either missed fish or are wild. It is estimated that 30 percent of the steelhead in Lake Ontario are now wild fish. I like the idea that I am fishing a wild-steelhead stream.

I call my friend Joe from Oregon. He will remain "Joe from Oregon," which may protect his identity some. Joe is one of the most hardcore West Coast steelhead guys (who often call themselves Metalheads). He encouraged me to use a Spey rod for the first time. I tell him about my little stream. I tell him because in the past my invitations to fish Eastern steelhead have been met with anger and disdain—mostly because it was a stocked fishery and he feels the experience is a mockery. I thought that the invitation to fish my little stream with its wild fish would be the ticket. As small as it is, I have had ten-fish days there. I wondered how long it's been since Joe had seen a ten-fish day? The last time I fished with him, we caught two fish over three days. I did notice this was considered good and it was part of the new paradigm on some of the Western steelhead rivers. I didn't mind. Fishing with an old friend is one of life's simple joys.

So I laid it on thick about my stream. I gave Joe the used-car salesman treatment. I told him about all the wild fish. The pretty little stream. How it has a Pool Five when there are only four. That we would have it all to ourselves. I thought I was making some headway with him. Then he just blurted out, "Look man, I am never coming East for steelhead. I will for whitetail or brown trout but fucking steelhead have no business there!" I sensed I may have gone too far.

I have other friends out West who have similar feelings. There is a big difference between Eastern and Western flyfishermen. It is a cultural thing with roots running deeply into geography and history. Whenever I fish the West, I always feel like a stranger in a strange land. I love it. It always feels new and brash and craggy. When I watch a Western guy cast a fly line, it is so pretty. It almost makes me want to cry. I can usually tell where a guy is from by the way he casts.

I sit and think about my conversation with Joe for a while. I know he is pissed at me, but we are friends and I also know in a couple days we will be okay again. Grumpy old men have a code. I am in my library reading *Winesburg, Ohio*. When I read I often have music on in the background. Johnny Cash comes on. I love Johnny Cash. I was lucky to get to know him a little when I was in the entertainment business. This song is "Hurt." If you have not heard it, you need to. The video was voted the best music video of all time.

I remember getting a call when it came out. "Hey, Johnny made a music video. I'll sent it to you. You have to look at it now." Okay, it sounded urgent, so I looked at it. I was stunned by its overwhelming power. I knew the song. It was written by a man named Trent Reznor. It was about the anguish in his young life. The song had suicidal overtones when Nine Inch Nails recorded it. It was probably Reznor's best song. Now Johnny Cash infused it with a hard life's worth of experience. Made a video to the soundtrack that chronicled his life—and in ways, every life—to the point of overwhelming. It is what artists are good at. What about Trent? These were very personal feelings. How did he feel about his opus being commandeered? He said: "I pop the video in, and wow . . . Tears welling, silence, goose-bumps . . . Wow. [I felt like] I just lost my girlfriend, because that song isn't mine anymore . . ." I wondered if it was like that for Joe about steelhead. If he felt like he lost his girlfriend.

I think I have a feel for the way some of my friends feel. I hope in the end they realize these fish are really their "children." I can see a scenario in the future in which some of these Great Lakes fish are sent home to California and Oregon and Washington and British Columbia to help rebuild the decimated stocks there. In my heart, I would like to see both East and West fisheries thrive. I am a fisherman and the more places I can whip water, the better I like it. I have stopped bugging Joe. He has promised to come out for some fall brown trout. He may accidentally hook a steelhead. It happens all the time. That will be in the hands of the fishing gods and that is where I will leave it.

I love steelhead fishing as much as any other kind. For a dry-fly guy like me, that means a lot. A ten-pound-plus steelhead hooked in a small stream is fishing's version of a cage match. The setting is usually very quiet. I like fishing in solitude and steelhead are conducive to that. You can catch them all year but the fishing is really seasonal. The fish start coming upstream in waves in September with the weather, and continue all through the winter. I fish for them in every month of the winter. I have one rule. I won't break ice off eyes—mine or any on the rod with which I'm fishing.

There was a day this past October. I love bow hunting in October. If I can get in a tree stand with the foliage on fire and that crisp punky smell of the morning, it is everything. This particular morning had that snap in the air. Just a touch of frost on the grass. Not the killing frost, not yet. It was pre-rut and the young bucks were randy as hell. Chasing does all over creation not knowing it was hopeless. There was a buzz in the air. The earth was electrified. Nature was plugged in and wired for sound. Sitting in the tree stand, I could feel the juice emanating right out of the ground. I could feel it resonate in my chest. It was all happening and I was tuned in and I knew it. Instinctively, I could feel her coming. I grabbed my bow. Sure enough, the big doe floated through the opening toward my stand. It was over seconds later. It was perfect predation.

It wasn't even 8:30 a.m. when I had the doe hanging from a tree. The cool fall air eased into my lungs. I thought about going to work. I thought about going fishing. I do not often mix hunting and fishing days. I know there are places that advertise cast-and-blast packages but I think they are better sports for separate days. I am not sure why. It is like going from beer to liquor. It can be done, but I just don't. Well, not often. The thought of hitting the office on this day just felt wrong. Blue sky, no wind, cool, and the electricity was still pouring into me. The internal debate was short. I gathered up my gear and headed to my stream.

When you open my steelhead fly book you might see a sea of orange with a splash of pink here or chartreuse there. Egg patterns are all I fish. I can tell you that not all eggs are what they are cracked up to be. I have become somewhat of an expert on egg patterns. I have some favorites. I did for a long time resist the use of synthetic materials, but that barrier eventually came tumbling down.

I sneak into the Oak Orchard (New York) fly shop and buy a credit-card-limit of some fine epoxy eggs. I still fish the natural materials when I decide to put bamboo in peril. A steelhead on a bamboo rod is Russian roulette for the wood-like fly rod. (Okay—bamboo is actually in the grass family, not wood.) When I have that traditional itch I tend to go traditional right down to the fly. Some friends tease me and suggest that I should invest in silk line. I don't have the heart to tell them I secretly did. In case you are contemplating it, drying silk line is slightly less fun than a colonoscopy.

I finally get to Pool One. I like this pool a lot. There are times when you can see the fish stacked up. Big visible fish can cut both ways. If they are active, it is the ultimate thrill in fly fishing. Watching a ten-pound-plus fish take a fly is bliss. On the other hand, having them ignore repeated presentations can be maddening. Worst of all is doing something doltish and spooking them out of the pool. This is the first of the four pools. There are some pockets between in which a blunder will spook out 25 percent of the day's chances.

I can see the fish; there are a couple of big hens in the pool. I make a couple of inadequate casts and on each a fish follows for a short time. They are not aggressive but seem to be workable. I decide to work the tail of the pool. If I hook one, I can lead it to the bottom of the pool and maybe not spook the rest. If you are a steelhead fisherman, you are probably already laughing. If you are not, that's like saying, "Maybe if I light this stick of dynamite in the backyard no one will notice." You certainly have a better shot than if you light it in the front yard, so you try.

After a half hour of more careful casting than the first few I made, the line stops. I pull back on a solid object. This fish, without any coaxing, does exactly what I want it to do. It swims methodically down and out of the bottom of the pool without disturbing the other fish. I remember thinking, "Damned cordial!" Then it kept moving down. I tried to turn it. It kept moving down. I was into my backing and the fish was pulling hard as hell. This fish didn't jump. All steelhead jump. I keep following the fish down. After a while, the stream begins to deepen. I know what that means and I look up. There she is—Lake Ontario. I followed the fish a little more than an eighth of a mile to the lake. When I say "followed" perhaps you have romantic images of the priest scene in the movie *The Quiet Man* or the wonderful scene of Paul Maclean holding the rod over his head rolling over rapids in *A River Runs Through It*. This was more "*Three Stooges* bank-dick chase scene" with all the slapstick elements. The stream does not have neat trails and in spots the shoreline is as slick as snot.

With the lake in sight, it seemed prudent to pick a bank and work my way to the shore of the lake. I managed this with some dexterity. I actually gained some line on the fish. As I reached the shore at the side of my little stream, I had gained back all the backing. I had steady pressure on the fish. I decided to add a bit more pressure, to tire it out. The additional pressure induced additional will on the fish's behalf. The fish started moving out with determination. I added more pressure and the fish responded with more determination. This was a cause-and-effect relationship that I knew would have a very short shelf life. I looked down as my backing dwindled. This fish was not turning. I was fishing a stout 7-weight with an 0X tippet. This fish was not turning. My backing was gone. I pointed the rod directly at the fish, which produced that high-tensile tone of good mono stretching to its limit. Then the crack. That was it. I never saw the fish. It never jumped.

I have sat around talking about what it could have been. The New York record steelhead is just over thirty-one pounds. I don't think it was a steelie. It would have showed itself. Some say if they get too big they can't jump. The New York record brown trout is just over thirty-three pounds. I never caught one on that stream, but why not? The record king salmon was almost fifty pounds at that time, with much bigger ones netted. Sturgeon grow into the hundreds of pounds. Why not the Loch Ness Monster? Lake Ontario is massive. It is 193 miles long and 53 miles wide. Only your imagination limits what can swim in there. I have had several mind-blowing experiences on the lake. This one was a pretty good one. If he had gone upstream? He would have run out of water in a hurry. I probably wouldn't have landed him but I might have seen him. Maybe it's better that I didn't.

I go back to the pool. Why quit fishing over something like that? Besides, the trembling in my hands might impart just the right action to the fly. Mending my line a little closer, hands a quivering mess—if you have ever lost (or for that matter landed) a giant fish, you know what I mean.

On the mend, the egg pattern gets a strike and I strike back. It seemed a bit light and I caught flashes of yellow and green. I was thinking this is so odd. I pulled the striped fish from the water. It was a large yellow perch, the kind we call "jack perch." There have been times in my life I have hunted these down. Yellow perch are delicious—cousin to the walleye and every bit as tasty. This guy was three quarters of a pound. I started laughing to myself. I never expected that. I sent the egg pattern along a similar drift and it got hit again. Another jack perch. I was still grinning from the first. My mind was wondering if I could catch a mess of them, enough for a fish fry?

It's funny how an event can trigger memories from deep in the corners of our minds. Thinking about the perch made me remember my grandfather. He was where my fishing began. He passed it to my father when I was very young and started giving it to me. He never fly fished, that would have been too much folly. He was a child of the Great Depression fishing to procure food (although fun had a purpose). Catch-and-release of anything edible was unthinkable. His whole generation shared a kind of frugal no-nonsense attitude. Add Catholicism and the meaningful place that fish held at dinner on Fridays during Lent, and the fish were never getting off the dinner plate. Being a consummate fish killer and eater, he had a favorite: the yellow perch. If he could have his way, small yellow perch were the best. They would be gutted, scaled, deep-fried, and eaten, bones and all. A little lemon and Tabasco sauce *s'il vous plait.*

I watched the fat yellow perch swim off. I sat there for a moment in the essence of my grandfather's persona. We hold a type of limited immortality that lasts until the final remnant of someone's memory of us dissipates forever. I decided to leave that pool and come back at the end of the day. To come back and catch a perch dinner for Abe. Fillets, that is—not bones and all, that still sounds bad.

The next pool was smaller and deeper. The water flowed directly onto a big boulder. The water deflected around the boulder into the pool and eddied. The best strategy would be to cast above and let the fly drift down to the pool. On the third cast, the fly stopped, and I pulled back. The reel exploded and the steelhead tail-walked across the pool. Minutes later, I released a beautiful seven-pound steelie. A few casts later the line tightened again. This was a peculiar fight. Strong and digging. I lifted and the fish resisted. It was like trying to pull up a garbage-can lid. Several minutes later, the stubborn fish finally gave up. It was a channel catfish. I started to look around. I was wondering if there was a hidden camera somewhere. What the hell was going on? The best I could tell was that the electricity I was feeling was flowing through everything. I had never caught a channel cat in that area, and I never, ever caught one on a fly rod. I could probably try for the rest of my life to catch one on a fly on purpose and *not* do it. The day was becoming surreal. I enjoy it when we seem to become a character in a backdrop.

Here I was in this place all alone. I could always imagine a fishing show similar to Charles Kuralt's *On the Road*. The camera pans in on this picturesque little stream. The shot swings around and you see this distinguished-looking middle-aged flyfisherman laying out a beautiful cast. The noise of the place is amplified for the viewers. The babble of the stream, the honking of the migrating geese, the glorious twitter of the songbirds. The camera pulls back to capture it all. There it is, the money shot. The fisherman sets up on a nice strike. He fights the fish valiantly. Then he pulls out a beautiful . . . channel cat. That might be a tough script to sell.

I did appreciate the turning kaleidoscope of the day. At my age, I have found that surprises are usually bad. When the phone rings and you are fifty and someone on the other end says, "Guess what?" You're usually thinking, "Oh, fuck." On a day on which I can have several surprises in a row and have them turn out harmless and pleasant, I am pleased.

I fished the rest of the pools and caught two more nice steelhead. One was a ten-pound fish. A day when you kill a beautiful deer and catch-and-release a ten-pound steelhead is really something. I keep days like this in my hip pocket. I trot them out on the bad days to remind myself that I do have it good.

I started to think about my West Coast friend Joe again. And then the Johnny Cash song. I wondered to myself, was this my empire of dirt?

Trent Reznor wrote the words as an angry young man and the despair is obvious. Empire of dirt to him was a disdainful description of a bad place in life. It was powerful and poignant in the way youth knows. When Johnny Cash recorded it, he transformed "empire of dirt" into life's accumulation of possessions. That in the end it means nothing. We leave with what we came with.

I think my empire of dirt is the moment of grandeur I can coax from nature. That the memories I make each day afield are my empire. It changed the way I hear the song, forever.

Chapter 4:
Munsungan

"Faith is knowledge within the heart, beyond the reach of proof."
—*Khalil Gibran*

My father asked me, "So do you want to come back here for a week next year?" I told him I did and he asked me if I was sure and I told him I was. *Here* meant a week fly fishing in Maine's North Woods in September. Sounds so simple and in some good ways it is. Some very good ways. The trip to Maine's North Woods, to Bradford Camps to be more specific, was to indulge my father's latest obsession: Eastern brook trout. To be more specific, Eastern brook trout in their autumn spawning colors. These are considered by many anglers to be the most beautiful of all trout (even if the brookie really belongs to the char family). Its olive sides with pale, often yellowish spots and red spots with lovely blue halos. The sides are orange to red moving toward the belly with black borders on the fins. I understand his obsession. I share his obsession. His obsession is mine. It comes to me in a linear genetic fashion. Through me to my children. The obsessive genes not necessarily the same kind. The gene itself is a bit troublesome. In its expression it can be rarely good and really bad. I watch my daughters with concern, I police myself with vigilance. Even when it manifests itself in a seemingly harmless fashion like fishing, there are problems. Not the same as if single-malt Scotch and blondes were involved.

Currently I am being tortured by bamboo. I like bamboo rods. I always have. Not just fishing with them or buying them. That is not enough. I want to build them. It is part of the control thing, the obsession: I need to get it just right and to control my part of it. I started with graphite blanks. That didn't cut it.

I had been talking to a friend, George Maurer, who made wonderful rods. He also was a good teacher. He was going to let me take his class. I finally signed up. George had a heart issue and we never made a rod together. I regret missing that. George was a master. If you get a chance to throw a fly with a Sweetwater rod, you will understand my regret.

Now I look online all the time. There are talented rod guys out there. I need the right guy. Learning from the wrong guy—fuck. After missing out with George it has to be the right guy with the right stuff. I know I will end up with twenty or thirty rods. I will get there. Eventually. It will be right. One channel of a fishing obsession.

My father has been obsessed with Maine and fly fishing for almost a quarter of a century. He retired there. His little town's biggest claim to fame is that Ted Williams used to love to fish there. For years, the passion was smallmouth bass on the surface with poppers. There is a cabinet with tens of thousands of poppers. One of my pure joys in life is to sit there in front of that cabinet with a fly case. Slowly and methodically going over the poppers. With many, I can tell who made them by the style. I just like to see the drawers. All the colors and feathers. One by one, I build a fly box for the coming days of fishing. It is easy to share obsessions with the people we love. It explains how some unimaginable things come to pass. Sitting in front of all these poppers, I can understand how Frank and Jesse James turned bank robbing into a family business.

The following September came and I made my way to my father's place in Northern Maine. Looking at the sky and listening to the Calais, Maine, weather report. Calais is not terribly close and the weather reports from there are often different from the weather we get. The problem with being in the middle of nowhere is you have no weather report. You rely on the closest place that does. Think about how unreliable your local weather is. Once removed from civilization is that much worse. The good news—a large high-pressure system was dominating the Northeast for the better part of the week. It made me feel good because the next morning we were going to catch a floatplane off the dock.

I like floatplanes. There are many reasons why I do. They are such a romantic icon for the wilderness experience. In my mind, it symbolizes a detachment from civilization. On a simpler level, it means better fishing. If fewer people can get there, it has to be good. What that really means is we have been conditioned to the fact that people fuck things up. If too many people get to a place, they fuck it up. In short, people are bad for places.

I hate to admit it, but I agree with that. In my lifetime there are way more of us. The changes have been stark. We have developed the hell out of everything. Somewhere in the process we developed a soulless environment. Any place of an appreciable size looks like any other place of similar appreciable size. We used to have regional flavor and tradition. Americana was fun to find and see. Now we have been homogenized. Just like milk. I could blindfold you and take you down the commercial drag in Fort Wayne, Indiana, or Youngstown, Ohio, and you would not be able to tell the difference. The Walmart, Burger King, McDonald's, Walgreens, Auto Zone, and all the rest of the soulless zombie mind-numbing corporate conformity. As each day passes these corporate pricks figure out how to eke out profit margins from and in smaller and smaller towns. Killing the remnants of Americana and the American dream all at once. In the smallest and poorest parts where the corporate codpiece cannot figure out how to cop a buck, the old diversity hangs on. Usually those same corners are where the good hunting and fishing and the people who would not be homogenized end up. I find myself gravitating toward these places. Often in floatplanes.

Standing on the dock on a cool crisp fall morning waiting for a floatplane stirs me. I hear the distinct drone of the single prop. There are three of us. My father, his wife Pam, and me. Pam doesn't fish. She loves my father. Loves hanging out in the North Woods with him. They are good together. We load up the plane. It is a Cessna 206 series. It is a wonderful four-seater on which to mount pontoons. It fits the people and all their things quite well. It is nice to get on a floatplane and not see the pilot adding up the weight in his head. It makes me feel a bit safer.

I like watching the pilot. In this instance his name is Jim. I have taken enough flying lessons to be a bad passenger. I have finally learned just not to talk. I watch and talk inside my head. Good enough.

As the plane picks up speed, Jim pulls back on the stick. It is a perfect blue-sky day and the plane lifts effortlessly. In an hour, Munsungan Lake comes into view and some tiny specks that I know to be Bradford Camps.

The Bradford Camps are not new. In fact they are very old as fishing camps go. Bradford's roots reach back into the 1890s. In all those years, the camp had been held with pride in very few hands. The hands that hold it today are those of Karen and Igor Sikorsky. If you are wrinkling your nose at the reading of that name you have good reason. Igor Sikorsky was the Russian-born immigrant who changed aviation in the U.S. (and the world) forever. Among his achievements were designing and flying the world's first multiengine fixed-wing aircraft. Bradford's Igor was this Igor's grandson and namesake. The camp is proud of its connection with aviation history and it is integrated into the camp. Igor and Karen are integrated, too. It turns out this works rather well. Karen once worked in advertising and marketing. Igor could not fight his predisposition and was a pilot. They somehow met. I am guessing at a Grateful Dead show. In the North Woods, they have created this wonderful bohemian outdoor thing.

Bradford Camps comprises eight guest cabins and a lodge. The guest cabins are old and built of logs. They consist of a wood stove, propane lights, beds (with wonderful linens and pillows—in the wilderness this *is* a luxury). A sink, flush toilet, and hot shower. No television. No Internet. There is a telephone if you must. Half the point is to unplug from the world. When I was growing up we didn't have cell phones. It amazes me how we have become so dependent on electronics so fast. I actually love unplugging, I call it Jerry Unplugged. It takes two or three days for it to really set in. On or about the third day I begin to really slow down. (If this gets out people could actually be hard to reach.)

There is also something very retro about reading an actual book under a propane lamp. The light has that yellow-white hue. It gives the reading a *film noir* quality. It has become so enjoyable that I play into it with my selection of books. Next time I am going to bring *The Maltese Falcon* by Dashiell Hammett. Sitting in the quiet cabin reading next to the wood stove. It is late September and so far north the woodstove is needed. The nights are cool, sometimes into the twenties. I love burning pine. The smell and the occasional sharp crack as the sap ignites. Munsungan's resident loons give their haunting and lovely call. You pause and take time to let your mind wander. You think about the fishing. This is just the perfect backdrop. You came to fish. Like a painting. It is the whole canvas.

At 7:00 a.m. the triangle is struck with energy. It beckons to all the cabins. Breakfast will be served in the main lodge. The day begins. I get up and feel the chill in my cabin. I look at my woodstove and wonder if I have any embers left. There was a time when keeping a fire in a woodstove was a meaningful skill. If you had it you enjoyed comfort. If you did not you alternated between freezing and sweating. As I peered into the stove I looked at the ashes. The trick is to build up a nice thick bed of embers. One that will radiate an even heat all night. I run the poker through the ashes searching for hot embers. I wonder what will be for breakfast. I never eat breakfast at home. When I get to a lodge it is a real treat. I am hoping for pancakes. I would never prepare them for myself so they are an even more splendid event here. I did well: There are some live embers, enough to ignite wood. I wonder if I will make the week without having to light a match in the stove. It is a kind of woodsman's challenge. I will say nothing but in my heart I will keep track.

The lodge is a warm and incubating place. There is a sitting area around an old stone hearth. I am told Jimmy Buffet is a regular. I have never run into him here. It is easy to imagine him playing a tune by the fire. I cannot say if it ever happened. Igor keeps a nice stock of flies and Munsungan swag. I always buy other guys' flies. I purchased a shirt for my Dad. Next to the sitting area is the dining room. Each party sits at their own table. Far enough from the next table for it to be private. Close enough to answer how the fishing was. The meals are always wonderful. Igor and Karen have a large well-kept garden. Much of the food served comes from that garden. You see the staff picking fresh corn on the cob and you just smile. Karen's marketing is sharp and on point. It is okay because it is righteous. Things here are intentionally kept close to the earth. Even the ice in your glass was cut the previous winter and stored in the ice house. None of this is an accident. Igor is a maniac. He stashes a beer every few feet in the ice house just to keep his cook "in it." Some of the guides claim they have to break things every so often to keep Igor sane. The place is in perfect condition. You can see his grandfather's genes bursting forth.

The place Igor Sikorsky can be seen the clearest at Bradford is in the air. One of the great features here is that you can book a fly out every day and fish a different pond. The winged chariot that takes you there is Igor's Cessna Skyhawk. It is green and white and looks and sounds like perfection. It is this part of the business that my father came for. It is by daily fly in that he will go after his latest obsession. Fall North Woods brook trout. It is here where our paths diverge. I love fall North Woods brook trout. I was hoping I would catch some of those beautiful works of art. Dad would fly alone. I was going to stay and fish Munsungan. I had fished it the year before. I fished it very briefly. Just long enough for my obsession to creep in. I waited a year to sate it.

The year earlier, I found out that Munsungan was full of native landlocked salmon. I fished the lake on a day on which the weather was poor. I had finished chemotherapy a few months earlier so with the dicey conditions I wanted to remain near my cabin. I had trolled my fly line and hooked several salmon. There are those who will say that trolling a fly is not really fly fishing. I hate those purist assholes. To hear them talk just kills me. Often they know little or nothing of the sport they claim to be experts in. I can usually spot them a mile away. They are usually tackle snobs. They throw around names of people they never met and brands they paid too much for as a means of legitimizing themselves. I guess if that's what it means I am glad to be an illegitimate fringe player.

I could have noted that trolling for landlocked salmon is quite old and steeped in fly-fishing tradition. That men were dragging flies behind boats in lochs across Scotland many years before someone paid way too much for those waders from Orvis.

My guide introduced himself while I was admiring my pancakes. I was admiring not just the pancakes but the honest to goodness local-made maple syrup. You have to boil down forty gallons of sap to get one gallon of syrup. A sugar maple had to bleed deep and long to sweeten this stack of cakes. Yet I had absolutely no regrets and was enjoying the rare treat. So much so that I almost missed the introduction to my guide. When I looked up and saw the maw that drawled hello I was pleased. It was Dick Mosher. There are names that have status in fly fishing. Guides can be some of the best celebrities that a mostly obscure sport has. The Maine guide is a legendary appellation. Dick is a legendary Maine guide. I had no idea this was the man I would fish with. I had heard he was starting to cut back a bit. It was said he was taking no new clients. He would work with the ones he had for years. He told me he had taken the liberty of tying his canoe to the dock in front of my cabin. All he needed was a time we were going to start. I said, "Eight-thirty."

At 8:30, I went down to the dock. We loaded the rods and my fly bag into the canoe. We set out trolling all morning. Dick was very talkative. I enjoyed it very much. He told me he had just recently turned eighty. That he was supposed to go home for his mother's birthday but Igor talked him into staying to guide me. He was starting to cut back and I was his first new client in a long time. In fact he no longer guides clients, just old friends. He was a retired math teacher who had taught high-school algebra and trig. How he would have never made it now because the equations shared time with hunting and fishing tales. Over the course of the week he kept me full of those tales. Not an easy task as they were good and my appetite was always ready for more. At eighty, he could paddle the large squaretail canoe with ease. He loves it. His affection could be felt with each stroke; finding out the canoe was made by Dick helped to bring it all together.

The best thing that can happen between a guide and his client is that their relationship develops a certain ease. An understanding of what the fisherman is after. The best guides get it and as long as it is fair, they try to accommodate. I was with a legendary guide.

Dick asked me what flies I wanted to fish. I handed him a box of tandem-hooked salmon flies. He told me that they would work but bait and lead-core line worked better. I told him I knew. These were the flies I wanted to use. The box had tandem streamers. There were 9-3s, Black Ghosts, Allagash Al's, Blacknose Dace, Cynthia, Grey Ghost, Green Ghost, Mickey Finn, Pink Lady, Silver Doctor, and a few with regional names and patterns I have long since forgotten. I knew this was not the most accepted method here. It was the method I wanted. It was my obsession. I wanted to fish these beautiful flies. I wanted to fish these flies for landlocked salmon in a way that has been done for a very long time. Trolling these patterns off long lines behind a wooden boat. I love these flies. I buy them when I can. Sometimes just to look at them. Pulling them through the water, they are supposed to look like a smelt. A small baitfish that salmon love. These flies come in limitless patterns. Just like fly fishing in a stream where a subtle difference in a fly can translate into wild success or utter failure, salmon will be finicky to the point of madness. This is why I am here in the boat with Dick. He knows it and we fish it. I am a casualty to the art of seduction.

I hold the rod as we troll. Munsungan is a big brooding lake. It has deep holes that harbor lake trout. There are brook trout here too. I am holding the rod for landlocked salmon. The turning leaves and cool nights do tell that the fish should be thinking about procreation. There are inlets into Munsungan. We stopped here and there. I have a 4-weight, two-piece Winston rod that I am partial to string up for the occasional session of casting. Mostly we troll. When a salmon hits the trolled fly it is incredibly hard.

A jarring stiff and solid jolt to the shoulder. The run is fanatical. Strong and swift.

When you do see the fish you cannot understand how it was not so much bigger. How, for its size, it created so much action. Then you think it through—it starts to shine through what vicious predators they are. It is honest blood-thirsty survival. They are the top predator in this water. They know nothing of your sport.

As I fought one to the boat, I looked at it differently. I noticed the design forged on evolution's drafting table. Its compact torpedo-shape body was put together for power and speed. There is no stocking in Munsungan. To me wild fish look, well, wild. I do not have any issue with stocked fish. Side-by-side, wild fish just pop. They are masterpieces. A reproduction only pales in the presence of the original. Thankfully we rarely see the two side-by-side.

Dick and I fished like this for most of the week. There was a soaring high-pressure system stalled over us. The fishing was marginal. You hear the term "blow out" for days like these. Many have tried to tie weather conditions with fishing since man first put a string on a stick. For myself I am not so sure. In my years all I can say from my experience is that I have had some good days on a falling barometer. All the rest fails to really hold truth as I recall some fine days with a sapphire-blue backdrop. I am sure there are some who have studied the shit out of this. In truth I really do not want to know. I like a fresh start every morning. Enough days are ruined just by plain old bad weather. I don't need science jading the rest. If fishing is poor it only means the fish were not hungry. Why they are not hungry becomes a strange science. Unless it leads to a way to make fish hungry.

My father was not having great success. The other fishermen at the other tables at meal time were struggling as well. Dick and

I were doing by far the best. We were fishing different but we were catching fish steady all day. As the week wore on, more guests were switching over to trolling flies. It seemed we would leave a spot and they would roll into it. They would see us boat a fish and they would mimic our effort more closely. Yet in the evening in the dining hall, the results they reported were not great. My guide was the best but I knew it was more than that. I am a pretty good fisherman but I was just holding the rod. It was because of Superman. We were catching fish because of Superman.

Superman is the name I gave my tandem streamer. I was not sure what its real name was. I purchased it years earlier at a gas station/fly shop somewhere in Cape Breton. It was basically a Mickey Finn with a bunch of blue hair tied in on each side. I had two. One really got chewed up pretty well; the other I took back home to use as a model and get more tied. My fly guy thought it was a local variation. In my tandem box its name is Superman. For the week we tied on dozens of different flies on a second rod and had very little success. So unless you had the quirky oddball fly, fishing stunk. It is this quirky quality of fishing I love.

Dick and I kept trolling the inlet of the various streams. We knew that in time the salmon must obey the urge. The urge of sex is universal. It is the drive of all things. Man has tried to mask it. Usually the repression leads to horrible results. Nowhere else is there the attempt to control what nature has hardwired. We knew that at some point it would happen. It being that event window where the forces merge and it all comes together. Where it is like someone turns on a switch and the fishing is great.

Sometimes it can last for days but more likely it is measured in minutes. If fishermen where naked in their honesty (something very difficult for us all) they would admit it is these brief flashes that drive us. Sure the usual success is good. All the nuances that outdoor writers have been capturing for years matter. The payoff is different. It is these moments of lightning in a bottle. At the heart of the sport is this belief that it will happen. No science or predictable schedule. It is faith-based like religion.

Dick and I talked about it for a while. Dick smiled and said, "Faith is knowledge within the heart, beyond the reach of proof." I said, "Gibran, right?"

I love it when a couple of seasoned outdoorsmen connect on an intellectual level about faith-based intuition in the middle of the wilderness. As if a cue was read a fish rose twenty feet ahead. I looked at Dick as I grabbed my Winston 4-weight. I checked the knot that fastened an orange-and-white Bomber to my leader.

It was a nice cast. Maybe a foot from the concentric rings pushing outward. A moment passed and then it was smashed. In the net it was a pretty squaretail (brook trout) of about sixteen inches. Rises started all around. There was no visible hatch. I kept the Bomber on. The next fish hit hard and jumped several times. It was a different fight, it was a different fish. A sturdy landlocked salmon was at boat side.

For the better part of an hour, I cast to rising fish—never sure what it was until the hook was set. One time a big brook trout, the next a strapping salmon. My first Bomber was completely unraveled and the second was getting there.

A fish would rise and Dick would work his eighty-year-old arms and position the canoe perfectly for each cast. During that time no words were spoken. A guide did what he had to do, the client's casts were reasonable, and the fish were turned on. This is it. Every article of faith must be rewarded for religion to be secure. I have had these moments and they are rare and different. Here I was catching brook trout and salmon together cast after cast on Munsungan Lake. I was high on the altar. Through it all in the back of my mind I could hear the drone of Igor's plane. I knew my dad was on it coming back for dinner. I looked over my right shoulder and I could see the green-and-white Skyhawk. I turned back to the water and it was over.

Chapter 5:
The Dinner Rush

Sometimes situations arise in ways all their own. There is a place near Lyndonville, New York, where this has happened. The spot is a triangular apron within which stand three large trees. These trees are covered with shoes. For years people have been throwing their old shoes in the trees in some sort of ritual. Over the years, it has taken on a meaning of luck. The trees are now known as the Lyndonville Shoe Trees. In fact, you can Google "Lyndonville shoe tree" and see what they look like. Even my own daughters have felt the need to apply their unneeded footwear to these poor arbors. This has been ongoing for almost three decades, Most people do not know why. The people who started it have moved on. It accidentally became something else.

I am going to dispel the magic and explain how the shoe trees came to be. It was part of a road rally sponsored by a college in nearby Rochester. At the time, there was a food stand that had an ice cream cone sign out in front on the main route. I am sure the directions said, "left at the ice cream cone." The runners went right at the shoe tree. At the time there were four pairs of antique shoes nailed to one tree. Spray painted on the road was an arrow and the letters RIT (Rochester Institute of Technology). Now, many years later, the ice cream cone is gone and the paint is gone, but hundreds of shoes fill the trees. The lucky shoe trees are an unintended byproduct of human nature.

The Grand Lake Stream Dinner Rush is similar. The Grand Lake Stream, Maine, that I talk about is both a place and a stream. The town of Grand Lake Stream sits on the banks of Grand Lake Stream. Both are located in Washington County, Maine. To avoid confusion, I will refer to Grand Lake Stream the town as the town and respectively I will refer to Grand Lake Stream the body of water as the stream.

Misunderstandings usually take time to resolve and evolve. This case is no different. In my youth, fishing came to me at a very early age. We would leave Cape Vincent, New York, on trips to regional places to fish. The main force behind these trips was my father. There were often other combinations including his father and various uncles and other folk. The focus of our attention was smallmouth bass. In the late 1960s and early '70s the motto of our town was "Cape Vincent Home of the Black Bass." Black Bass being at that time just another moniker for the smallmouth bass. For various reasons, we ended up leaving the Cape. The fishing had declined and, in a way, so had our family.

In the years that followed, my father would still go on the occasional fishing trip. Then he just stopped. At first I was troubled with it. I just couldn't understand how you could walk away from it. I am not being sanctimonious; I just couldn't see how that was possible, in the framework of having similar DNA. I would try to talk him into going here and there. Sometimes it would get thin. One summer we were on tour together with our entertainment clients. We were taking a break out in front of a theater. The conversation came around to happiness and quality of life. I told my father that he seemed less happy the further removed he got from the only true hobby he ever had, fishing. I think he got angry at me, at first.

But Dad is a smart man and things started to change. He went to find his smallmouth bass again. We went on some interesting fishing trips to find the right fit. Eventually Dad landed in the town. When I say "landed" I mean he is one of the hundred or so year-round residents of Grand Lake Stream, Maine. He has retired and has become a full-time bamboo bum. He has become the best fisherman I know. It is a long way from the front of that theater.

The town has become a second home of mine. It was a long circuitous road to get there but I haunt the place pretty good. One of the nice things is that for such a small place it has more than its share of history. One of the local legends is the Grand Laker. This is a canoe that has been developed locally and by evolution of design and craftsmanship is greatly desired. Often getting passed from father to son. Mine is treasured. They are light and large. Tough and quiet. A flyfisherman's dream. Most of my time here is spent in a canoe going from lake to lake chasing bass. That's the funny part of it because the stream is often considered the finest landlocked-salmon fishing in the world. To drive the point home a little better, my cabin overlooks the Dam Pool. This is probably one of the most famous salmon pools in the world. I watch guys fish it from my porch after a long day of bass fishing. I know, I know, I get it all the time—I never fish the stream. I think part of it is because I like solitude. The bigger part of it is that I really dislike Orvis assholes. It is to the point I avoid conversations with them when I can. I know they mean well but so did Stalin.

There does come a time when the kids go back to school and the stream is still open. That's when the summertime catalog-model fishermen are back in the office. There are still guys on the stream but they are the guys I don't mind. Some of them take a walk after dinner in the same wool pants and flannel shirt they did thirty years ago. They have been through several changes of the guard at Weatherby's (the fishing camp in town) and practice decent etiquette on the stream. The stream itself is legendary, its pools and spots are known by name—the Dam Pool, the Tree Stone, the Wall, the Hatchery Pool, the Evening Pool, the Glide, Big Falls, Cable Pool, Little Falls, Big Eddy, and more. That's a lot for a little more than three miles of stream. I like to fish it in late September. It allows me to say, "Of course I fish it." The fishing is good and it is past the bass time. Being Down East in late September is something in itself to experience. So much is going on. The leaves are putting on a show. The locals are switching from fishing to hunting. Things are starting to quiet down. That is a relative term. They are quiet by most standards but it can be downright slow. I think the hundred people who stay in town look forward to the deafening silence. My dad does.

In my twenty-plus-year association with the place comes an association with a man. Louie is a licensed Maine guide whose life has got tangled up with ours. He spends most of his time helping us keep our part of this place right. More than that, he has become a close friend. We are about the same age. We are both pasta-loving, gun-toting, fly-fishing Italian sportsmen. In the state of Maine there are exactly two of us. Over the years our lives have run down parallel streets. It lets us talk about family and life situations in an earnest and private way. It is like having a brother you choose. If he happens to be a Maine guide, well, that is so much the better. We have spent many days in the canoe together. Every year we talk about some of the same things. One of the topics is always the grouse. I love grouse hunting. It goes back to a simpler time when I lived in the Catskill Mountains. I always want to know how he thinks it will be. Grouse populations can vary wildly and some of it is cyclical and some of it is caused by spring nesting conditions. The conversations always end the same way. "You ought to come up and we will hunt them. Come up the last week in September and fish salmon and then stay for the October 1 grouse-season opener."

I always say I will but life is popping at home, too. I am an avid bow hunter. The local streams are filled with giant brown trout. It is sometimes easier to stay home. You always tell yourself that you will go someday. Someday can get away from you. I was also concerned with staying close to work. If something comes up and you are close, you can just go to work. Some would argue that that might be a good reason to go away. I've always had a driven work ethic. Those close to me say I am stone-cold Type A. I am working on becoming Type B. You could say I am using my Type A drive to become Type B. Some Type A people would say that what I am trying to do is impossible. I know in most cases that may be so. I do have some hope. I have a calling. Like a man joins the priesthood because he hears an inner voice. My calling is not so pure. I can be distracted by things outside. The secret pond or valley of the giant whitetail deer. The trick is to keep moving from one project to another. Of course, you could argue that you are being Type A about Type B.

I decided I would come to Maine the last week in September and stay through the first week in October. I would drive up. Packing fishing-and-hunting gear is a lot for a plane. The potential for devastation in the event of lost luggage is mind-staggering. With the drive, you run into Massachusetts' draconian gun issues. I would purchase my ammo in Maine but taking a gun into communist territory is a bit touchy. In checking with some savvy folks, the most prudent advice was to gas up in New York and drive right on through. Luckily, Massachusetts is a small state and you can get past it in little over an hour. Ironically, my gun has killed fewer people than one of the Bay State's favorite sons driving over a Martha's Vineyard bridge all liquored up. Mary Jo Kopechne would have been way further ahead grouse hunting with me. Guns and all.

After I settled in at my dad's, Louie came over. We chatted about the fish-and-game laws. Although you could fish the stream until October 20, the last day you could keep a fish was September 30. Grouse season opened up on the first of October. Right off the bat, the hunter-gatherer in me had the calculation. "So if we do this right we can have a Grand Lake Stream surf-and-turf feast on the first."

"You getten lowbsta?" Louie asked. I had made a mistake. If you say surf and *anything* in Maine it means lobster. Lobster was cheap enough that we could. But that was not what I meant. "Look, if we do this right we can have salmon and grouse and Maine potatoes on the first. Like a local feast!"

"What about the lowbsta?" Louie asked. He was on point about having some bugs there too. (Bugs being the slang name for the arthropod, lobster.) Why not? Everyone likes them. It was decided. We would have our special fall feast. Game dinners are getting to be popular. This would be a little different as we were counting on the freshest ingredients.

The week of fishing started off wonderful. The crowds were small and polite. The fishing was good. Louie would check in. He would ask if I kept any fish. I would tell him not yet. That we wanted fresh. It was about fresh delicious game. The fishing kept getting better as the week wore on. Louie would come in and see if I kept anything yet. Of course I hadn't. "You know there's a chance the weather's going to turn," he said.

"I've been wet before," I said. "I was born that way, you know." I was being cavalier and cocky. It can happen to even the most seasoned angler if he gets on too good a hot streak. Boy, was I *smoking*. It was all I could do not to show off by casting behind my back and between my legs. It was so good that the other fishermen were shaking their heads and moving away a bit. I like that and tend to enjoy it as it is a rare occurrence. I am usually the guy you see wrestling with a waterside bush trying to get his fly back. There have been times when I have left enough flies in a tree that it starts to look decorated in a Christmas sort of way.

My plan was to keep my limit on September 30. Word about the feast had got out and invitations were extended. Lobster can do that. I now had to recalculate the haul. I would need my limit on September 29 and 30. Sitting and thinking about it made me a bit nervous. The morning of the 28th was going to be serious business. I was going to pay attention to what I was doing. I took a pen and a note pad with me. I wrote down what I saw and the strikes and fish follows. What flies were doing what. I did great that day. The sun was on my face. The leaves were at peak color. The salmon mugged my fly all day. They jumped liked they wanted to be on a magazine cover. I wanted my karma to be good with the fish gods and I released every fish unhurt. I felt so good I quit early. I sat on my porch watching the other guys fish. I went over my notes and put my gameplan together. I refined a beautiful fly box. Lining each fly up by type and size. It was a masterpiece. The kind of thing that might disturb some guys. I put on a new leader and cleaned my line. I was ready and happy. I went down to the Pine Tree store for a turkey club sandwich with extra bacon. What the hell, I was feeling good. I read a couple of chapters of *Atlas Shrugged*. Usually I am a night owl. Most nights I am awake well past midnight. Insomnia is a family legacy. I was feeling so good here, that I felt sleep coming on early. I was in bed at 10:00 p.m.

I am not sure how REM sleep works in other people. It never seems to come up in conversation.

"How was your REM last night?"

"Oh man, I had some fucking REMMERS let me tell you!"

My REM sleep is random and deep. If a disruption comes during REM, it takes a while to get through. Even the alarm clock going off—I hear it in the corner of my consciousness. I am not sure for how long. I hear it for a while before I know what it is. Then it takes more time for me to decide if I am going to deal with it. Then I have to decide how. Sometimes the how is a process taken over in my alter ego. When he decides it can suck. Over the years I prefer to leave my REM alone. It was during my REM sleep that I heard a knocking. I heard it deep. Then my thoughts began to work. "Who the hell is knocking? What fucking time is it?" You push your state of consciousness to glance at the clock on the nightstand. "*Three-thirteen?*"

The next question is: Three-thirteen what? You look at the edge of the blind. To take a peek outside. It is dark. Three-thirteen in the morning.

Adrenaline shoots into your system. Someone knocking at your door at three-thirteen in the morning is trouble. I sat up. Rolled my feet out of bed. There was the knocking again. I got to my feet and ran to the door. I put on the light and opened it. No one was there but all hell had broken loose. I heard the knocking again. It was a tree limb banging against the cabin. Rain was coming sideways from the sky. Trees were swaying and bowing like young people in a mosh pit. It was a Nor'easter. They had called for a chance of rain. This was a surprise. I made some hot chocolate and turned on the weather channel. Some storm front moved in, in an unexpected way, but the European model did show that this could happen. In the end, with billions of dollars worth of satellites and hardware and software updates, weather is unpredictable. I went back to bed.

I woke up the next morning and the picture from the window was not a pretty one. It was raining with fury. I was in a quandary. I wanted to catch my two fish. I needed to catch my two fish. At times such as this we start to make rationalizations. "It's not raining that hard!" I don't know why but I wondered if Noah ever said that. I laughed at that thought. I would wait it out. In the afternoon the rain did let up a bit. I put on my waders and went to the Dam Pool. I knew it would fish like shit. I could see it from my porch. I tried anyway. The water was high and debris-filled. It was as close to unfishable as I have ever seen it. I gave up. We would see what the next day would bring.

More bad weather was in store the next day. We would have no salmon at our feast. Someone mentioned we could go to town and buy some salmon. That was more offensive than going without it. This would just be another store-bought meal. The idea was to put on a hunter-gatherer feed *extraordinaire*. We had our principles but they were wilting against the clock. October first came and the grouse hunting was poor, as well. Louie's dog had a hell of a time with all the water. All the birds we saw were in trees. Finally out of desperation I had Louie shake a tree. As the grouse flushed, I knocked it down with my 20-gauge. It is not how I like to hunt them but desperate times call for desperate measures. That grouse would have the honor of being the only fresh game present at the First Annual Grand Lake Stream Dinner Rush.

That evening, we had a wonderful dinner. We ate the steamed lobster. There were genuine Maine salt potatoes. I had sliced the grouse breast thin and served it with a Marsala sauce served over linguini. We had lots of fine wine and nice backround music. It was a pleasant and cozy evening. After enough wine had flowed, the men folk got together and created the rules for next year's Dinner Rush. They were discussed and debated and when a consensus was reached they were jotted down on a napkin for posterity's sake. The main rule was that as much of the food as practicable had to be gathered on September 30 and October 1. That participants must fish for salmon and hunt for grouse. This rule has been amended to allow one guest for each participant. The dinner has expanded and is something we look forward to. Wild blueberries are hunted for pies and mushrooms are sought. The lobsters are still a big deal.

It has reached the point where some of the newer participants have no idea how it started. We used to make them swear on the napkin but someone blew their nose on it and we threw it away. Now you have to bring a bottle of good wine to join. The event has become important to me. I mark the time off as soon as I buy my planner every December. This past year, I had someone ask what I was doing for some of that time. I told them that I had to do this Dinner Rush thing.

"You could miss it once," she said.

"Oh no. It is just not possible," I answered through a smile.

"Everything is possible," she insisted.

"I just can't," I said. "I must follow the inscrutable exhortations of my soul!"

"Oh, that is so good," she giggled.

"I know," I said, still smiling. "I stole it."

"From who? Hemingway?"

"No, a guy named Bill Watterson. A reclusive cartoonist."

I guess when you start quoting a cartoonist whose claim to fame is that he disappeared more completely than J. D. Salinger, the conversation is over. As for the Grand Lake Stream annual Dinner Rush, it goes on every year. Like the Lyndonville shoe tree, it has become something different than what it started as. People like to have events and observances that bind them together in a spiritual way that is easy to do. In a world in which *easy* is getting more difficult all the time, that is not a bad thing.

As for our dinner, the biggest challenge is the salmon and grouse. Sometimes we have too little or no salmon; sometimes we have no grouse. Once in a while, it all works out and we have plenty of both. Those years are special. Grace means that much more.

Chapter 6:
"Plucky, Game, Brave":
Smallmouth Bass
in Three Parts

"The black bass is eminently an American fish . . . [H]e has the faculty of asserting himself and making himself completely at home wherever placed. He is plucky, game, brave and unyielding to the last when hooked. He has the arrowy rush and vigor of the trout, the untiring strength and bold leap of the salmon, while he has a system of fighting tactics peculiarly his own."
—*Dr. James Henshall, Book of the Black Bass, 1881*

PART I

When someone asks, "What's your favorite fish?" you usually have to sit and ponder. I have thought about the question repeatedly. It is like someone asking about your family: Which child is your favorite? The question cannot be answered. I could give my favorite ten fish. I do know the fish I spend the most time pestering. *Micropterus dolomieu* is its Latin name. *Micropterus* means (in Greek) "small fin." *Dolomieu* is after Deodat Gratet de Dolomieu, a French naturalist and geologist whose good friend Lacepede first described the fish. Sometimes the proper name of a species sheds some light or provides insight. In this case, the name provides very little. In fact, the fish's scientific names are misleading any way you tug at them. This is not a bass but a true sunfish. His mouth is not small, it's just smaller than that of his cousin, the largemouth. Even the other names given to it—bronzeback, brown bass, brownie, smallie, bronze bass, and bareback bass—just miss all the way around.

Being a nine-year-old boy in Cape Vincent, New York, and chasing smallmouth bass was a matched set. I was just starting to get sophisticated. I was determined to be the greatest spin fisherman who ever lived. I knew my stuff. I had a 5-foot, 8-inch avocado green Garcia Conolon 8229 rod with a Zebco Cardinal 3 spinning reel in two-tone green that matched nicely. When I wasn't on the water I was in my yard tossing lures into cups, ashtrays, bowls, anything that would present a challenge. To this day, I can still put it on the money with a spinning rod. It is one of my many talents that has no applicable use today. I shouldn't say that. I still spin fish on rare occasions. I love to catch walleyes and don't do it nearly enough. So it is a vestigial skill that does serve me well when I get to use it.

There was one evening I was throwing an Abu Reflex. An Abu Reflex is an old spinner-type lure. The one I was using was orange with black spots. It had a silver spinning blade and a treble hook below the blade. The treble hook was covered nicely by dyed orange feathers. It was an effective lure. Not only was it flashy, but it also had a certain vibration to it. On this particular evening as dusk was settling in my young eyes, I noticed a smallmouth bass feeding on the surface about twenty yards away. This was new for me; I had never seen, or noticed, this before. At nine, distractions are many and focus is never easy. The bass was feeding toward me. I wondered what would happen if I threw the lure right on his nose? I made the cast and the lure did not even get a chance to spin. The bass hit as soon as the lure hit the water. I set up on the fish quickly and he was on. It turned out to be one of the best fish I had caught in my early angling days. I thought the whole event was spectacular. I shared the story with anyone who would listen. As I told the story to the man at the hardware store where I had purchased my hard-earned tackle I was enlightened by him that this kind of fishing rewarded precision; that it was beautiful and genteel and steeped in tradition; that it was considered by many to be the truest form of fishing; that when I was ready, the hardware man would help me put together a fly-fishing outfit that would rival the spinning outfit I had. I would have to shovel about the same number of driveways that winter. I wondered why I had never heard about this fly fishing before?

It wasn't that fly fishing was novel or new; I am not that old. It was just considered quirky and those who did it were the eccentric fringe of the fishing fraternity. When I ponied up at the counter with my hard-earned snow-shoveling money, I had no idea what lay ahead. The nice man who took my money for the spinning gear was eager to take it again. It was a Fenwick kit that contained a fiberglass rod and a reel, line, leader, tippet, and flies. Those early days of fly fishing were dark and awkward. There was no Internet or fly-fishing school. I remember checking out a book from the library. It was a book written in 1920 by a man named Larry St. John. It was called *Practical Fly Fishing*. The book was "sympathetically dedicated" to "The Women The World Over Who Have Been So Unfortunate As to Marry Men Who Go A-Fishing." I am sure there are some who think that I am making this up but I am not. I can tell you the book is dead serious about the sport, and the dedication is in tune with the whole book. To this day, I am not sure if the book helped or hurt my efforts in fly fishing, life, and relations with the opposite sex. It didn't matter; it was the only book on the topic at the time. I was the only person to ever sign it out. I can say that with confidence.

I can say that with confidence because I still have the book. With the nickel-a-day library fine it puts what I owe on the book at roughly seven hundred dollars. I can tell you it is not a seven-hundred-dollar book and so it will remain underground with me. In those days, as I say, there were no fly-fishing schools and if you didn't have family members or neighbors who fly fished you took what you could from Larry St. John. "Foreword: Here then is 'Practical Fly Fishing' a companion book to my 'Practical Bait Casting,' and like that little work this is offered mainly as a text book to help the novice through the places where there is rocky, rough water, and other hard wading. It will be noted that I have devoted more space, proportionately, to fly fishing for black bass than have other writers. . . ."

I remember thinking this was so great. Larry St. John would be my fishing guru. I would often start off fishing platitudes with the phrase "Larry St. John in his book *Practical Fly Fishing* would often say (or do) . . ." and it would then sound reasonable.

Larry and I worked out my earliest challenges of fly fishing. You had to be credible to be published, right? By the time I was a freshman in high school the book had become somewhat dog-eared. I had read it at least a dozen times. My parents in their loving Catholic way decided on nine years of Catholic military school for me; then it was my time in college, during which I finally became a decent flyfisherman. I got accepted to a small liberal-arts college called Hartwick College. It was located in a small city called Oneonta, New York. I had no idea what to do with my fly fishing or maybe subconsciously I knew. Like I said, all fishing is local and here I was nestled in the Catskill Mountains.

I could be in Roscoe, New York, in just a tad under an hour. It was during my time there that I met Lee Wulff. I remember begging several flies he tied off him. (He would not sell them to me.) Several weeks later I had them in a beautiful leather fly book and asked him to sign the book with a Sharpie marker. He asked, "Why the hell would you want something like that?" He knew why. Fly fishing was a small quirky brotherhood and it had few heroes. In some ways it was like a caste system (pardon the poor pun). There were a few at the top. I remember the first time I saw Joan Wulff cast a fly. I had to sit with my head in my hands for an hour. It didn't matter that she was a woman. I had never seen anyone throw like that, ever. The trout fishing was legendary in the Roscoe area. There were what we thought of as crowds on some of the streams. Today, we would pay and sometimes do to have that kind of elbow room. To get a break from the perceived oppressive crowds we would fish the Susquehanna River that flowed right through the center of Oneonta. It was jammed full of fat smallmouth bass. As small a fraternity as fly fishing was, the elitist element was there. There were guys who would get pissed because you were fishing bass with a fly rod. I remember about the first time I heard about a nut who was fishing the river just downstream in Pennsylvania. His name was Bob Clouser and he would fish for bass almost every day.

It was during these years that I went into my first *bona fide* fly shop. It was in Roscoe and all they sold was fly-fishing stuff. I remember walking in and not knowing what to think. It was there I saw my first rack of bamboo rods. I had seen bamboo rods used on streams. I had heard the talk. Graphite was pretty new and some guys were whispering about boron but it always went back to bamboo. I had never touched a bamboo rod. I wanted to but you really had to know someone well to ask if you could handle his cane rod. Now there I was in a fly shop with a whole rack of bamboo rods I could touch. I remember thinking, "Holy shit, these are slow!" It takes a while to understand what that really means on the water. There in my hands was this Paul Young semi-parabolic 5-weight. I remember thinking, "Do I want a used rod?" I sat in front of that rack for hours. It was something to be able to hold a bamboo rod. Price became important to the decision. I made a deal with the owner for the Paul Young rod. I gave him twenty-five dollars. I would bring in twenty-five more each week for the next four weeks and the rod would be mine.

I fished that Paul Young bamboo rod hard for the next two years. As it always does, life moves on and I graduated college. I left the Catskill Mountains behind. Somehow I always look over my shoulder for those mountains. On occasion I drive through them and all the memories and ghosts come flooding over me. To be honest, it can be difficult to feel them. I tell myself I will retrace some of those steps. I am not sure if I would be able to bear it. I could move there but visiting might be too hard. It is the land where Rip Van Winkle fell asleep. I know the story is allegorical and I get it.

PART II

From the time I was that nine-year-old boy throwing that Abu Reflex at that stocky smallmouth until now, I have been after the experience of catching top-water smallies. In the last two decades I have been going to Grand Lake Stream, Maine. I ended up owning a place there and a Grand Laker canoe. I can keep myself occupied with hunting and steelhead fishing. But no matter what I do, February comes to my life. Cabin fever is a nasty time. I had some friends talk me into ice fishing. It turns out that's what married guys do to get away from their wives and do a little drinking. The guys I went with didn't even drill a hole in the ice. I said, "Hey, screw you guys! I'm not even married, I can drink at home if I want. Shit, you guys can come over. We'll watch the outdoor channel and I'll turn up the heat." Instead, I spend the cabin fever days dreaming of going to Maine to fly fish for smallmouth bass.

Louis Cataldo is a Maine guide and family caretaker, of sorts. More than all this he has become a friend. He is as steeped in the Maine woods as a man can get. His father was a guide and his mother was an author. His grandfather was Hill Gould and shot the buck that has stood as Maine's non-typical whitetail record since 1910. Some folk know when they see the year's first robin or the first crocus that winter has given up. I know when I hear Louie's Down East accent that bass season is close. I have been out at home fishing for a few weeks with the trout people. I enjoy the early spring with them. That is early April and May. Around my home it is primarily a 3-weight affair. All the while I know I can get snowed out. When I head north with a 5-weight, I figure I finally made it to another warm season.

Recently, I tried to figure out how long I have been going to Grand Lake Stream to fish for smallmouth bass. It has been more than twenty years and fewer than thirty. I looked at some photos of me with bass and without wrinkles on my face. The seasons stack up like cord wood. The bamboo rods have stacked up like that, too. It's a long way from the Paul Young 5-weight. I sometimes fish graphite now when the conditions are raw out. I find it is a bit easier on my casting shoulder. I played football and lacrosse hard and I feel those days more now than I would like to admit. It is easy to sit and wander through the years and memories. It's nice to have a place to serve as the backdrop to help gauge the years. You remember things like the rainy year I got divorced. The year I broke my favorite rod on a big bass.

Grand Lake Stream has always been tied to the outdoors. The history of fishing and fly fishing there goes back more than a century. In its earliest days the area was full of brook trout and Atlantic salmon. The landlocked salmon were like a boutonniere on a tuxedo. It was beyond what you wished for. A fishing nirvana. It was a bad time for ecology. The lumber companies cut timber without regard—using the rivers and lakes to transport the cut lumber. The locals and tourists killed all the pretty fish they could and would never eat. In the end, the fishing gave out. It happened in lots of places but here, in Grand Lake Stream, it was everything. When the fishing was gone, everything was gone.

Nature in the long run can be resilient. Laws were enacted to stop the paper companies from laying waste to the watersheds. Responsible management allowed the land to heal. Somehow the smallmouth bass found its way into the vacant niche. There are lots of stories. I imagine the truth involves milk cans (used to transport fish for stocking) and Jack Daniels (used for the usual reasons). The bass spread out to all the surrounding lakes. That is the real greatness of the place. There are thirty-something lakes that I fish within an hour of my house. You can look at the wind or the weather or just because you have that "special" feeling and decide which place to go to. Some of the lakes are very large and some are just barely twenty acres. It doesn't matter where you go, the boat landings and the lakes are clean. The people are also protective of their fish. They act like someone who has had a second chance. I like that about Grand Lake Stream.

PART III

My father's place is about a minute from mine in Grand Lake Stream. In the town it is hard to get farther than a minute from anywhere. We tend to fish a floating block of time anywhere from late May until early July. It depends how the seasons go that year. Sometimes the spring will come early and everything moves quicker, sometimes it's late. We try to get to the bass when they are bedding up during the spawn. It's nice with all the different lakes in the area because the fishing turns on at slightly different times. My father likes to fish with a guide named Dave Irving. I like to fish with Louie Cataldo. Sometimes we fish the same lake and stop for a shore dinner. Sometimes we won't. It has been this way for a long time.

One of the things I do during the ugly cabin-fever times is to buy poppers. I am on eBay and web sites. I have tried to quit but my father does the same thing. It is genetically hopeless. I always get excited when I find something new or ugly. Often it is both new and ugly and I am temporarily happy. These flies eventually make their way up to the popper drawer. I know it sounds quaint but it is a sickness. If we could anthropomorphize a smallmouth bass and he could see the popper drawer it would disturb him deeply. Mother bass would tell their fry about it to scare them into behaving. The popper drawer must house, conservatively, five thousand poppers. I don't know how it happened. It is partially about the fear flyfishermen have of running out of that "one" fly. Even with such a hoard, it happens. There was this little off-blue popper. One season it was on fire. We had a dozen of them. They were gone so fast. Turns out the guy who made them had to go to prison. We even tried to send him the material to tie up some while he was in the joint; I figured he would have the time. Turns out the state of Alabama didn't want to help us out. We sent the last one we had to someone else to duplicate but they weren't the same. We laugh and say we will have to wait three more years for our big-house poppers to come in.

One of the lakes I fish in the Grand Lake area is half in Maine and the other half in Canada. Lately it has been very good for smallmouth. So good that many of the Maine guides have been fishing it pretty steadily. It is a big lake. If you are from the area you probably know the lake. If not, it really doesn't need any more attention or fishing pressure. It keeps producing wonderful bass. I keep waiting for the other shoe to drop. Eventually the word gets out. Then people move on. Years later it bounces back and the cycle (if that's what it is) can start all over again.

It was a beautiful day and the dragonflies were flying all over the place. I told my father I would meet him by the boat landing. As Louie and I pulled in, there were about a dozen canoe trailers at the landing. I said to Louie, "Let's go fish the American side." It was about a forty-five-minute drive back down. Louie let me know it had been many years since he fished the U.S. side. It wasn't like the Canadian side. It had a fair amount of development with camps and cottages. I told him I wasn't too concerned and I would rather hit shorelines that were fresh and unfished.

When we pulled into the American boat ramp, it was empty. The same lake, just a different end. If the fish at one end were so inclined they could swim down to the other end. I know the quality of the fishing can be different but at the same time it is the same lake. The fish don't need passports or enhanced licenses. They could simply swim over. Even if one side could be better, it wouldn't be *that much* better. You work with logic to get to a point where you can justify getting back in the truck and backtracking all this way, forty-five minutes. Backtracking logic has been an affliction deep-rooted in humanity. If it works out, nothing more needs to be said.

The fish cooperated right from the dock. I like days on which you know how it's going to be early on. As we fished out in front of camps you could tell that the fish were fresh. I had been noticing at the other end of the lake—the Canadian end—the bass had lost their eager edge. It always happens when a fishery gets a bit too educated. Some guys like it like that. I like it as forgiving as I can find it. In this life, I seek forgiveness, it's habitual.

It was a good textbook day. We caught double-digit numbers of bass. Not in weight, in numbers. Most of the fish were handsome bronze fighters in the one- to two-pound range. Though you start off the day sharp and concentrating, as the numbers mount, the intensity gives way. Your field of vision grows and you throw fewer casts and look around more. I like getting to that place because in a way you've stopped fishing and now you're outside. I love being outside. As a child being punished entailed taking the outdoors away from me for a predetermined length of time. Like eternity. I know every generation bemoans the next. It truly is part of the changing of the guard. I can't help but think this next generation today is a little different. As a parent you naturally go with the methods the previous generation used on you. It really didn't matter how bad life screwed you up. If you looked close enough you could identify some families by their particular psychoses. Sending my children to their room for eternity was akin to sending Brer Rabbit to the briar patch. In the end I had to adjust and banish them to the outdoors. Naturally, they were horrified. I recall watching one of my daughters endure the horror of her punishment outdoors on a swing. When she noticed me watching, she made a point to come off the swing and tell me what a terrible time she was having. In the end, she became a tree hugger. I am not sure what the moral of that story is.

Back on the American end of the big lake, we were just enjoying the day. Looking at all the cottages that mostly were not opened yet, Louie and I would discuss what our recommended renovations would be. In some cases a wrecking ball was in order. It was a pleasant day during which it was warm enough that you weren't cold but you didn't perspire, either. A lazy cast here or there. We were past one hundred bass for the day and there was light left. The shadows were getting longer. If we weren't in the canoe working our way back we might have said, "Today we caught enough." It was one of those days you have to remember and put on the right side of the scale. The other kind of day will come, as sure as shit. It helps to be able to say, "Well, yeah it was tough, but that day . . ." It's a Zen quotient. About forty yards up, I saw a bass working the surface near a solitary exposed rock. If the fish wasn't causing a ruckus, I would have passed by the spot. As Louie paddled the canoe closer, the feeding fish reminded me of that bass at Cape Vincent all those years ago. The memory drew a nostalgic smile to my lips. I threw the bug near the rock pile. *Bam.* As soon as the fly hit the water the bass took. She was a dandy. As I released her back to her rock I thought about things coming full circle. From that time to this and from that smallmouth to this smallmouth I have seen many worlds. I have become a decent flyfisherman.

Still, I can't say smallmouth bass are my favorite fish. I would have trouble with that. I can say that I have fished for them the most. That they might not be the beauty queen but rather the girl next door. After that fish, I broke down my rod. Louie paddled slowly and methodically toward the boat launch. I sat in the bow enjoying the colors of the evening. Some loons started their wailing. I thought more about that first bass. The journey I went on from that experience. How life can turn on a dime. There are times when it all just comes together. We have the urge to get cocky but if we resist it can become poetry.

Chapter 7: Africa

"If people bring so much courage to this world the world has to kill them to break them, so of course it kills them. The world breaks every one and afterwards many are strong at the broken places. But those that will not break it kills. It kills the very good, and the very gentle, and the very brave impartially. If you are none of these you can be sure it will kill you too, but there will be no special hurry."

—*Ernest Hemingway*

Sometime in August 2011, I was shaving in a nice hotel room on Prince Edward Island. I was on holiday and spending time with my family. That's the way it always is. It starts out innocuous enough. I felt a bump on the outside lower left of my mandible. It was smaller than a pea. I'm not sure why but it bothered me. I kept fingering it all through the trip. It was hard and immovable. I kept trying to remember if it was always there. I just couldn't recall. Things tend to stick with me and to be honest it stayed in my mind all through the trip. I would be enjoying myself and then I would touch my chin and that would be that. I decided to put it out of my mind and deal with it once I got home. It really didn't help except that I decided I wasn't going to ignore it.

When we got home, it was still there and still troubled me. I had decided to do something about it. I was wondering if I was silly because I felt perfectly fine. I knew I didn't really want to go to my GP. He had turned into a midlife-crisis mess. I liked him well enough but his head was not in medicine. It troubled me to no end. It was on my jaw near my teeth so I decided to go to my dentist. He was a sharp young man. I trusted him so I booked an appointment. He took X-rays and poked at it a bit. Told me it was probably nothing but he called an oral surgeon friend of his who was waiting for me. I have been accused of falling off of turnips trucks as recently as the day before yesterday. Having an oral surgeon waiting across town to see you usually is not about nothing. My dentist is a good egg. I smiled tentatively back.

I made my way to the oral surgeon, who was waiting for me. He took his own X-rays. Then he said he was going to biopsy the thing but it was probably nothing. So far that day I had heard it was probably nothing but they were going to take a piece of my head to test just to be sure. It was a tougher task then he imagined as he broke two scalpels getting it. He told me he took most of it and they would get my test back soon.

Two weeks passed without much sleep. Human beings have this large, self-aware brain. There are many instances in which it brings joy and really is a blessing. Its ability to worry about unknown outcomes must have some evolutional basis. I can tell you it did me no good at all. I started making calls to get the results. One of the conversations was to urge me to be just a little more patient. "Lady I am out of fucking patience. I have lived waiting for two weeks. Tell me who I have to shit on for my results." She kept giving me that *sir, sir* shit so I hung up. The next day I was driving home from a business meeting in Alliance, Ohio, when the oral surgeon called. He asked me how I was. Huh? I said, "fine." It's funny how we have the ritual of small talk. "I have your test results. I need to tell you that you have non-Hodgkin's lymphoma." He told me a bunch of other shit. I really didn't hear much of it. I pulled over and had to get out of the car on the side of the highway. As I made my way home, I had to deal with the fact I had cancer. Long drives are good for anguish. The miles can pound the anger out of you as good as anything. There were a couple of days of tears shared with family. In between, you get on the Internet and look up treatment and survival rates. You take in as much information as fast as you can. It is the initial confrontation of your mortality. You learn that it is a fast-moving cancer and you have to move as fast. I am lucky to have an aunt who loves me and has ties with the outstanding cancer hospital MD Anderson, at the University of Texas. She put her resources to work and found the best lymphoma guy was this doctor named Myron S. Czuczman. Turns out he is affectionately know as the King at Roswell Park Cancer Institute, about an hour from me. At least one of the most agonizing parts was made easier—where to go.

It was early October when I had my first appointment. They took all kinds of tests, including a marrow sample from my hip. When I met the doctor, he was a large, pleasant man with vibrant blue eyes. His bedside manor was so good. It gave some peace where none had been in a while. He told me that they were going to give me a test and stage me in about three weeks. He also told me about the cancer and what I was up against. That if I was not feeling the symptoms, I would soon.

As I left the exam room and walked into the lobby of the hospital, I saw it different. On the way there, all I could see was what I was doing. Now I saw all the sick people. So many, maybe two hundred, milling around the lobby alone. How could so many be inside this giant facility? All sick with cancer? Where did they come from? I couldn't get my head around it. Harder still was the concept that I had it too.

As I returned home, I had an answer to one of my questions. I could hunt and fish as long as I felt up to it. Bow season had already opened. One of the greatest joys in my life is sitting in a tree stand enjoying the autumn. Years earlier I had quit the bow when I found the equipment wanting. Maybe I couldn't perform well enough with what was available. For whatever reason, I didn't feel lethal enough. Seven or eight seasons ago I fell in love with the bow again. It was a whole new world and it fit me. It had got to the point where I will always prefer it to the gun. I felt relief that I could get into a tree if for no other reason than to collect myself.

The next morning, I was in my stand. It was a glorious morning. I had on a long-sleeve shirt and that was enough. The sun was rising on a cool, crisp morning. A doe walked right into my shooting lane. I drew my bow and set the sights upon her vitals. In the moment I could not fire. I let the string back making only the slightest sound. Nothing was wrong with her reflexes and she was gone. I was confronting my death and death in a broader way. I took the release off my wrist. I was going to have to work this out. I sat in that tree all day contemplating life and death. At one point I fell into a dry hacking cough. It was something I could not suppress. I knew it was the beast inside me.

The next morning, I did not feel like going to my stand. I did manage to get to it in the afternoon. I had my bow and several deer came under my stand. I did not pick up my bow. I had to resolve the question about death. Was there something that gave me the right to take life? I needed answers. I did something I had not done since I was young. I asked a higher power for answers. I have always been something of an agnostic. I think it was all the years of Catholic military school when the Jesuits kind of beat the Jesus out of me. This was not a full-on conversion, just more of a reaching out to a higher power. I now know prayers do not fall on stones. Yet I remain as suspicious of organized religion as ever. On that day, it felt good to ask for help. The dry cough returned, causing the little herd of deer that had gathered beneath me to flee. As the sun was falling I remembered what Hemingway said about death. How the world either makes us strong at the broken places or kills those who will not break. I wondered if the world would break me or kill me.

As the week wore on, I struggled with the question of death—and in doing so, one must deal with life. In the world there are some who are predators. They are who they are by design. They had no choice in the matter. On the other side of the balance are the prey. In a Zen relationship, together they create a web of life across the planet. Humans in the equation are different. After millions of years of evolving as top predator on the planet some have thought their way out of the role. That does not bother me. Maybe that is the next step evolutionarily. In searching my soul I just know that I was created in the traditional human role. I am a hunter, I was born this way and should be true to myself always. I came to peace with some things. That I am a fair hunter. I use what I take. That I am a child of the earth and like the things I hunt.

I was glad to have come to terms with it. I figured out that I was missing the morning hunting sessions because fatigue had really started to come on. I was getting winded walking the hundred yards from my four-wheeler to my stand. The cough was becoming more regular, too. The beast was growing fast. On this day it was cooler than before. It took more layers to stay warm. I wanted to live normal for as long as I could. I began to savor the time in the stand. As the light went low flocks of geese migrating south started to land in the surrounding fields. There is something very primal about the sound of the migrating birds. I am not sure why but tears flowed down my face. I sat in the stand until well past dark.

I said very little to my daughters about the cancer creeping along inside me. I wanted them to feel okay as long as they could. In my family there has been a tradition of venison cutlets for Thanksgiving and Christmas. It is my grandmother's recipe. She was always very closed-lipped about it. One year on my birthday she asked me what I wanted. I said, "I want to learn how to make your cutlets!" She looked at me crossways for a minute and grabbed my cheeks. "Smart boy," she said, "smart boy."

I have been applying that recipe to venison ever since. It has always been out on the plate every holiday for more than twenty years. It is nothing for fifteen to twenty pounds of meat to disappear. For some reason, on that day after my diagnosis, it became important to have venison cutlets.

Family rituals are important everywhere. They become more important in times of trouble. They somehow expose the roots that anchor our tribes and give the members a sense of self and security. Procuring the meat for our ritual also gave me a focus away from myself and the impending test results, which would lead to something I tried to keep far away. The stories of cancer treatment can be as terrible as the disease itself. I had decided early on that unless it was hopeless I would fight for my life. It isn't as natural a thought process as you would think. There are scenarios you play out where you quit, where you run out of humane thought and throw in the towel. In a way, this time between diagnosis and staging is a no man's land. You spend all this time walking around dealing with your own mortality. In cancer circles they call it "scanxiety." You spend a lot of time in bed looking at the ceiling. It is good to have a diversion even though nothing blots it out completely. It is like wearing earplugs at a gun range.

It was three days before I was going to get staged. The meeting where everything hangs in the balance. They tell you how likely you are to die and what they are going to try to do to save you. My walk to the stand had gotten harder. I needed to stop and rest in the middle. Getting up the ladder was getting harder. I had abandoned trying to set my alarm for the mornings. I would leave at 1:00 p.m. and get comfortable by 2. On this day, a giant 150-class buck stood broadside in front of me. It was the perfect presentation. I stood so carefully. My throat tickled but I used all my might to suppress the dry cough that was trying to start. I did my best to draw the bow. The cancer had moved enough to compromise my draw. Under great struggle and with shaking hands, I got the arrow back. I set the pin on the buck's vitals. As I released, the arrow flew off the string in a cockeyed manor. It went way wide. It was all me. I could not keep the draw correctly long enough. I kept on the stand and a doe gave me a similar shot at twelve yards with the same result. I was crushed. When I got home, I could not get warm. I soaked in hot water for hours. I would not hunt the next day.

As the morning comes for the trip to get staged, your mind goes crazy. I thought about making a deal with God. I thought how everyone must make a deal. I wondered how many deals get broken? I knew immediately that I was not going to make a deal. What did I have to deal with? Nothing at all. Instead, I made a deal with myself. I resolved that I would fight it with all my might. If I made it, I would go bow hunting in Africa. I could keep that deal. I would do my thing and God would do his.

If there is ever a time when a human knows and feels total humility it is waiting for oncology to stage him. I was trembling in the car ride to the hospital. I always thought I was brave. I found out, not so brave. As the doctor walked into the room, my hands were noticeably shaking. I was told that, freakishly, the cancer was just in my jaw and no where else. That I was Stage 1a. It was

October 26, a Wednesday. That I would begin R-CHOP chemo the following Tuesday. They prescribed me 100mg of prednisone to start the day before and to take for seven days. I would get the R part on Tuesday and the CHOP on Thursday. You stand there like you were hit between the eyes with a hammer. You sort out that there was some good news in there. The limited scope and early stage were good. The rest was in the paperwork. You get home and look everything up. While there is room for optimism there is a lot going on.

In a way, you absorb all the shock. It is a bitch. There is some relief knowing that treatment will start. You are not free-falling anymore. You feel like you are taking some control back in an event that was random and arbitrary. It is a little thing but it is something.

The next day, I went to my bow guy and had him take ten pounds off the bow's tension. I tried to sight it in but it was exhausting. I got the ten yard pin all right. The rest was a mess. I figured I would have to get close. I knew that with letting off so much in poundage maybe it was for the best. The leaves were mostly off the trees. This made it easier to see the deer. There were more deer that season than in the past few years. It made me think I had a chance. As the days passed and the chemo day drew near, it became more difficult to concentrate. My cough had become more persistent. Tuesday came and I had no chance at my deer.

Before you start your chemo, they ask you if you would like a port installed. It is a semi-permanent line to hook you up to the therapy drugs. It saves you from needing an IV installed each time. I declined to have one. I guess it is the stubborn streak in me. I wanted to leave there pretty much the way I came in. That Tuesday they administered the Rituxan, which is the "R" in R-CHOP. It was a bad hit right from the start. I had fever and chills all night. At one point, my blood pressure was 61 over 30.

So the fight began. I had the CHOP the next day and my white-blood-cell count fell through the floor. I would spend six days in the hospital. When I got out, I wasn't sure if I would get back to the deer stand. The cancer was the beast within and the chemo was the retaliation. My body was the battleground. The real issue is: Can you outlast the beast?

On Friday, November 11, I decided I would hunt that afternoon. I wanted to take a different route to my stand. I walked through a field I had been avoiding for four years. It was the field my good friend Don had died in four seasons earlier. I met Don when he sold me a bad boat. I went to check the boat and saw two brand new soft plugs in the front of the motor. I assumed anyone who would go to that trouble would have replaced them all. He assured me the boat was in "top shape." The second trip out into the middle of Lake Ontario, the old bad back plugs blew. I came crawling into the docks shooting water and steam everywhere. If it were not for a strong back, and a bit of luck, I would have taken out about a dozen expensive charter boats. I went to Don's house to share some of my pain.

As he came out to talk, I realized he must have been in his seventies. I couldn't choke him but he saw how upset I was. After a while, he agreed to help me with the boat. He was a retired charter captain. He never really helped me with the boat. I got something far better in the deal. I got a good friend and fishing-and-hunting partner. His own sons would not let Don hunt their land so I let him hunt mine. He was always at my house. Every morning, I could hear the door open and Don would start making coffee, although it would be hours before I was up. He would fix the leak in the sink or clean out the wood stove. Many mornings, he would be out manicuring shooting lanes. I always woke up to something. New tree stands, food plots, rod holders, anything he thought we needed. One year, I purchased an old StarCraft inboard/outboard to let him work on it. We nicknamed it the "Tub." What I can tell you about the Tub is that it was rebuilt in a mechanical sense. We purchased a new steering wheel and instrumentation. We refinished the wood in a dark stain and when it was all finished it looked like hell. How she looked (bad) was in contrast to how she fished (good). Don and I even finished fifth in one of the big salmon derbies on the lake. I can now honestly say I have been paid to fish.

During our friendship, Don was diagnosed with mesothelioma. He was in the Navy and had come in contact with asbestos. He would carry oxygen to the boat. As soon as we were away from the dock and out of sight of his wife, he would ditch it. Of course he would be quick to offer it up if I was fighting a Chinook for too long. The fall of that year, I would miss the opener of deer gun season to pursue elk out West with a bow. Don was out every day grooming the fields and checking his food plots. I would ask him if he saw anything good running around out there. There was nothing and he would be lucky to fill his doe tags, he would answer. I sit at the occasional poker table and his face made me look at him sideways. I figured I would be in New Mexico so whatever it was he wasn't telling me about, I hoped for him. The evening of opening day, my daughter called and said Don wasn't in yet. I looked at my watch and it was after five in New Mexico. I knew immediately; I told her to call the sheriff. An hour later she called back crying. They found Don dead lying next to the doe he shot. He knelt down to start field dressing her and never got up. He had a massive heart attack. They found him right next to her in a fetal position.

Here I was for the first time at the spot. I was winded when I had got there, so I sat next to where he went. I felt a chill breeze move up my back. I just sat there thinking: He cheated a terrible death with a fast one. He knew he was on short time. He put off surgery to be out here that day. I laughed because I remembered seeing the buck he was trying to keep secret. Then I cried about the feel of his death still at the spot. In a while, I was better. He got to do it right. We take our first breath and doing so we promise that we will take our last. Jim Morrison said no one gets out of here alive. Don surrendered the perfect way for an outdoorsman. He was just doing what he loved. I could feel death there, not just Don's or mine but all of it. My sentient brain grasped being gone. I have no idea if anything comes after. I just could tell that a day will come and I will no longer remember.

As I stood up, I saw something. I bent down to pick it up. It was Don's pocket knife. It was open and rusted solid. It was the blade he was using that morning. I put it back where I found it. I said to my friend, "I will remember you all I can." As I walked to the stand I wondered who would remember me. It is a profound thought. I changed forever at that moment. I am not one of those people who have an epiphany and sell all my possessions and do ministry work in Ghana. It was more a realization of time wasted. That our only chance of living for a while after we are gone is in the memorable times we share with the people whose lives we happen to touch. I worked my way to my stand. I managed to get up in it and somehow steady myself.

In the stand, the cool wind kept drying the tears that kept forming. I wasn't ready to leave. If it was my time, what could I do? I really wanted to stay and was more resolved to struggle. After a bit, a button buck started to feed toward me. Usually they are careless and as dumb as whitetails ever can be. In seasons past, I let them go to grow and become bucks. In seasons past, I was the mature lion with the full mane. Now I was a shadow of that predator. The season I lost Don, I had shot an arrow through an elk at fifty yards. Now I was hoping this deer would work his way to under ten yards. In years past the wait for the deer to come closer would have been rife with impatience and a keen predator's edge. Today it was with a sense of foreboding. I had no confidence left. The deer did get close. I struggled to pull the string. I was much weaker than when I had taken off the tension. Somehow the arrow found its mark. In tracking the deer to its final place, I had spent all I had. In the end my neighbor had been keeping an eye on me and showed up.

I managed to have the venison cutlets ready for Thanksgiving. I would have the rest of my second round of chemo the day after. It was not long after that all the hair left my body. When I say all I am talking eyebrows, eyelashes, the hair on my legs—even my genitals. I remember Christmas being at the end. Looking into the maw of the beast and not caring if I was done. Time pushes on and in its relentless turning, things must yield. In my case I finally had a PET Scan that was clean. Now I could begin the radiation. I would have five weeks' worth. Everyday Monday through Friday. But I would miss a day: I was going to the Harrisburg Great American Outdoor show in February. I had a promise to myself to keep.

The radiation phase was to ensure all the cancer in the area was gone. I was fitted with a mask that looks eerily like Jason from the horror movies. I would go every day and get radiated. After a while it causes a harsh burn. It was nothing compared to the chemo. You were assigned to one of four machines. Each machine had a waiting area. Everyone came the same time every day. If someone was on their last day, they usually had cookies or cupcakes. You felt good because it meant the end of their suffering, at least for a while. For some the process was much harder than mine. In my case it was a mopping up; some poor souls had the misfortune of having it be the frontline treatment. The scale was much different. On bad days someone would be missing without the cookies. We all owe a debt to death. I have no fear of it anymore. I hope for a good death. My fear of death has been replaced with a fear of life. Not life itself, but living the wrong life. I answer to my own conscience and only that. It makes life so much simpler and frees up lots of time to wander across the rock looking for the better fishing spot or the better tree stand.

Getting to Harrisburg was a little tough. I had not travelled since I went to Prince Edward Island. I had done some research and wanted to meet with this guy from South Africa. His name was Pieter Potgieter and he seemed to have a great concession in the Republic. I spent the better part of a day looking around the show. I met with Pieter the next day. I liked him right off. At this point I looked like a bad version of Uncle Fester from *The Munsters*. He treated me with dignity and understanding. He took his time and demonstrated that he was well experienced with outfitting bow hunters. I booked a trip with him for that May.

My recovery was slow. The doctors cautioned me that this was a remission. It would take being negative for five years to be considered cured. I lost saliva glands and have some permanent digestive-tract damage. A small price for kicking it. I worked my way back with my bow but I was by no means ready for the upcoming trip. I would make do with the recovery I was having.

Delta has a direct flight from Dulles in Washington, DC, to Johannesburg. As I boarded the plane, it finally sunk in. The world broke me instead of killing me, this time. I sighed a bit. As I got to Pieter's place it was wild and wonderful. In the evenings I could hear the hyenas call. The game was plentiful. There is something about the texture of Africa. It touches a deeply ancestral nerve. Theodore Roosevelt spent almost all of 1909 hunting in Africa. He felt similar feelings.

He wrote in 1910 about being in Khartoum: "The hunter who wanders through these lands sees sights which ever afterward remain fixed in his mind. . . . Apart from this, yet mingled with it, is the strong attraction of silent places, of the large tropic moons, and the splendor of the new stars; where the wanderer sees the awful glory of sunrise and sunset in the wide waste spaces of earth, unworn of man, and changed only by the slow change of the ages through time everlasting."

The hunting is from poured concrete blinds (called "hides") through much of the bowhunting concessions in Africa. It reminds me of a duck blind, in that you are at ground level. You look up to most of the animals. On the second morning we—Roche, the kind professional hunter, the trackers, and me—headed toward the hide from which we were to hunt. As I got out of the truck near the blind, the trackers went ahead to check. I smiled as I figured it was an exercise for the hunter's behalf. A lot like the grizzly-bear speeches to fishermen in our West. As I approached the hide, the two trackers busted out of there like a flushing pheasant: "Mamba! Mamba! Mamba!" they shouted.

I was back in the truck with the windows rolled up, the hair on my neck at attention, and my heart pounding in my ears. They went back in with sticks and dispatched the beast. It was more than twelve feet long. I have photos of the tracker holding the tail over his head while standing on the tailgate and the head still touched the ground. While I was in the truck dripping in adrenaline sweat, I thought to myself, "Do I feel alive!" It is not something I want every day but it was a needed jolt. That evening I took some ribbing about the lack of bravery. I laughed and told them I would have worn a tube top and lipstick if that's what it took to get in the cab of that truck. Yes, life was back to the same old crapola. It felt good for the edge to be gone. The next day, I shot a nice blesbuck and over the course of the trip I would take a super eland and gemsbock, along with a representative impala. My shooting was just fair. I would come back again with my skills in better shape, I told myself.

I have become a little more in tune with my body. I see an oncologist every six months. It is still a sword that hangs over your head. In cancer circles that feeling of where, when, or if it will come back is called the "noise." As I write this, it has been almost two years and I still hear it. It gets a little louder when you go for your scheduled test. It is there when you feel the little anomalies that pop up like a swollen gland. It helps you to look at your body like the tool it is. It helps you with life, too. I had always heard that the best revenge is living well. It is.

Chapter 8:
Cottontails . . . or Beating the Winter Blues

"I live in that solitude which is painful in youth, but delicious in the years of maturity."

—*Albert Einstein*

There are places in this world where the weather is always amiable. I don't live in such a place. My home is, and really always has been, for the most part, along the south shore of Lake Ontario—one of the Great Lakes. Still, it's difficult for most people to imagine the enormity of this freshwater sea. It takes getting into a boat and traveling far from shore so that land cannot be seen in any direction. The land surrounding each of the Great Lakes is usually low and flat, giving them the moniker "Lake Plains." Living on the Lake Plains has certain attributes that impact our lives. Water in its thermal state creates a large heat sink that affects the climate of the Lake Plains. In the summer, it offers a cooling breeze. Through the summer, the water heats up and to what degree affects those of us who live on these plains, sometimes significantly, for months to come. Buffalo, New York, (an hour west of my home) is legendary. Situated between two of the Great Lakes (Lakes Erie and Ontario), the lake-effect weather there in effect is doubled. Though the seasons are glorious and the lake itself presents us with world-class fishing opportunities, the winters can try a man's soul.

As cold Arctic air streams south across the lakes and collides with the air warmed by the heat-retaining water, the lakes become natural snow-making machines. Relief comes in some years if the lakes freeze quickly. Lake Erie being much shallower freezes regularly but Ontario's deep moody waters seldom freeze. Some years the snow keeps coming. As January moves into February, one begins to ponder the wisdom of ancestors who emigrated here. February is a cold and cruel month. Deer season and its many forms are done. Fishing is really more than a month off. I know ice fishermen will take exception to this. All I can say is it takes a special breed to fish on the ice. I simply am not one of them. I just don't drink like that anymore.

Cabin fever is a real condition. Some people call it the Shack Nasties; medical science calls it Seasonal Affective Disorder. Seasonal Affective Disorder becomes the cute acronym SAD for the not-so-cute affliction. The term I prefer is *winter blues*. I like the term "the blues." It sounds like what it is. There have been experiments showing that people who are deprived of sunlight and the outdoors get cranky. If things go on long enough, you have to alleviate the problem. In my neck of the woods, the answer was extending rabbit and squirrel season through the end of February. Not the solution for everyone but for an outdoorsman it is workable.

I have always enjoyed rabbit hunting. The Eastern cottontail makes for great sport and, in the right hands, exceptional table fare. As a young man, I was lucky enough to have my path crossed by such a culinary wonder. Her name was Molly Williams. She was the nanny of an old friend's cousin or something like that. I first met Molly when I was picking up my friend for a rabbit hunt. She made me promise that if I bagged two, she could have one. Nature was good that day and allowed me four and I gave Molly three. Molly was quite on in years back then. She was the great-granddaughter of a slave and carried on a longtime family recipe for Southern-fried rabbit. A couple of days later she made sure some of that recipe found its way to me. I shake my head as I write this. It was that good. Colonel Sanders has nothing on Molly. Our relationship lasted a good decade. Eventually, she helped me with the art of cooking a good rabbit.

Over the years, these late hunting seasons have helped with the winter blues. I enjoy the squirrel hunts in a hardwood. But as noble as it is, the squirrel has to take a back seat to the Eastern cottontail. Most hours spent afield for rabbits are with well-trained beagles. If you have not hunted this way, you need to—at least once. The baying of hounds putting the rabbits on their zigzag run until you get that wild shot is pure adrenaline. Real rabbit guys have kennels with a team of hard-working dogs. On those days when the rabbits are active and plentiful and the dogs are sharp, it can be pure action. I always love it when man and dog learn to work together on a hunt. Watching a beautiful English pointer set up on a pheasant or a hound on the chase is the pinnacle of hunting.

Dogs are like children. They need their people around. It's just no good to own a dog if you are going to be away from it. In my younger days, I had some handsome hunting dogs. On the right day I liked them better than most people. There will always be this one golden retriever in my heart, forever. I live alone and have to travel regularly. It would break my dog's heart. That's why I presently own two cats. They are both fat Devons and the only thing they hunt is me. They do like to keep me warm on cold nights. The best thing is they don't mind it if I am gone a day or two, here and there. Sometimes I even think they like it when I go. When I came home last week, the older cat seemed to ask casually, "Oh, you're back already?" Then went on with her business. I guess I'm in a cat stage in life. Not having a dog means I'm usually waiting for the invitation to hunt. Without that, I have to go on my own.

One of the regular escapes from the winter blues I have is solitary rabbit hunting. There is an abandoned railroad track near me. I can walk it for miles and the red brush that grows on both sides is good cottontail habitat. The old rail bed hardly ever gets used except by the occasional snowmobiler. When you are climbing the walls—the winter blues again—a nice long walk outside can heal some issues. This hunting tends to be just the opposite of hunting with hounds. It's slow and quiet and deliberate. Each footfall is heard and felt. The background noise eventually clears out and you are there with yourself. These long, cold walks gives you time to reconcile your life. It takes time and quiet to understand that some things may need an alignment.

Preparation is not involved. I always try to remember where I placed my old pair of Irish Setter hunting boots. I have purchased two pairs since. This pair is old and worn and stretched and comfortable. The waterproofing has given way. I rub a liberal amount of mink oil on the leather. I know I can wear several layers of wool socks if I have to. Diabetes has made it harder to keep the feet warm and more important than it used to be. Over the years, I have purchased miles of socks. All kinds of synthetics and blends. Some had batteries and some poorly chosen gifts had individual slots for each toe. Why is it gifts for outdoorsmen never work out? In my basement I have a singing bass, a singing trout, and a singing deer head. In that same storage area are four Ronco pocket fishermen. It is quite a collection. This year's Christmas presents could be the worst yet. I received a bunch of camo stuff. Not the good stuff, like clothes. I was given a camo flashlight, wallet, keychain, and knife. I am really not sure if people understand that good camouflage is supposed to blend perfectly with its background. Why do you want to give me things I won't be able to find if I drop? So off to the basement pile they go.

At the gun safe I ponder the firearm I will take on my hunt. The choice is really not too difficult. I have fifteen guns. To some, that may seem like a lot. It really is not. Like any other set of tools mine reflect the kind of work I do and used to do. There are a couple of muzzleloaders in there. The old New England fifty-four caliber is well worn and the classic style. I remember having to wait until the smoke cleared for results. In recent years I have fallen so in love with the bow that the smoke poles go unused. (Archery deer season and muzzleloader deer season tend to overlap.) I have two twenty-two-caliber rifles. One of them was the first gun I ever owned. I remember paying ninety-nine dollars for it and it being the most valuable thing I owned. One of the things you will notice looking into my toolbox is the left-handed tools. The higher-caliber rifles have bolts with left-handed actions. One, a seven-millimeter magnum, I won in a poker game many years ago. The guy was right handed so the loss to him was not great, but I wanted it badly. Living where I live, in flat low country (Lake Plains, remember?), the shotgun is king. We are even shotgun-only during deer season. My gun safe reflects that with the majority of the firearms being shotguns. I must admit to being biased about the shotgun. If there can be such a thing as a pretty gun, that would be a shotgun. Indeed, some are pure art.

My shotguns reflect who I am as a person. When you look you see that my youth was represented by power. I have a ten-gauge that will take your shoulder off if you hold it wrong. A great goose gun. The most represented gun is the twelve-gauge. Probably the most versatile gun ever made. Some have pretty etchings of hunting scenes. Then I have a couple of twenty-gauges and a sweet sixteen. As I get older, I lean toward the finesse of the lighter calibers. I love the sixteen but supplies are just getting harder to find and the range of shells keeps shrinking. More and more I grab for one of the twenties. Mine are both pretty guns. Both are nice Browning guns with the bottom eject that suits my left-handedness. So I pick one of the twenties and lock the safe back up.

I always clean and oil my guns when I take them out to hunt and again when I put then back. I respect my guns and want them to work properly. As I am cleaning the twenty, I start to daydream. One sure sign of the winter blues is the increase in daydreaming. I have always daydreamed. I can remember getting roughed up by nuns for doing it. Cautioning me that if I kept it up I would get nowhere in life. Perhaps a self-fulfilling prophecy from unhappy virgins in black? It's always a form of escape. This day I'm dreaming about escaping the winter blues. I am daydreaming that I am cleaning a Purdey side-by-side with all the heavy scrolling and etching. I have always wanted one but somehow a gun that cost that much (fifty to sixty grand or more?) just has not been a reality.

I find the hunting vest I like. It has a game pouch across the back. For the kind of hunting I am about to do it is exactly what I wanted. I grab a box of number six shells and fill the shell sleeves on the vest. The elastic in the cloth of the shell holders is a bit weaker than it used to be. I hold the vest in my hands. Memories of past days and hunts flood my mind's eye. I realize that I will soon have to have new elastic shell-holders sewn in. It's as if we somehow impart some of our spirituality into items that go with us often enough on intimate journeys. For this hunt, and for the next several, this vest will hold the shells and that is enough. I grab a small hunting pack that fits comfortably and holds a couple bottles of water, lunch, and a few other items. I round up everything and set it by the door.

I will try to go early in the morning. The only thing to do is check the weather.

I gave up on the Weather Channel a long time ago. It deals in general trends over broad regions. I want specific conditions in a very precise area. Several Christmases ago, a friend gave me a home-weather station. I was skeptical of the thing. It required being mounted outdoors and running power to it. Then you needed to mount and connect everything to the "station" indoors. I let it sit in the corner in a limbo of sorts. Nearly making its way to the "reject pile" in the basement. Its saving grace was that I happen to be a gadget junkie. One day two years after I had received it, I installed it. Turns out it works. If you use what it tells you (and your experience) you can do pretty well. It was reading a very cold twenty-two degrees. Wind chill made it minus ten. Rising barometer. I looked at the sky and it was clearing. The likelihood was a cold, sunny February day.

The alarm goes off. There is that moment when you have two minds and have to consolidate them. One is enjoying the warmth of the bed, and one is enjoying the anticipation of a long walk while hunting. As the clock ticks the confusion gives way. My legs roll over the side of the bed. My toes feel for the floor. The touch relays the cold and the one mind says, "See!" before it retreats into the reptile part of your conscious. I walk to the window and the stars are twinkling clear and sharp. It's going to be sunny and viciously cold. The local weather station and meteorologist do okay again.

I sit in a chair and wait for the kettle to whistle. Hot water is important. It's going to be tea and oatmeal for breakfast. With any luck the oatmeal will stick to my ribs for a while. Over the years I have hunted these tracks many times. Sunday morning at first light has been the established favorite. You walk for miles in almost perfect solitude. The God-fearing are working on getting to their house of worship. The heathens are stretching out the sins of their weekends just a bit longer. I am not sure which camp I am in anymore. I spent plenty of time in each. I was force-fed religion in my youth. So much so that I rejected it most of my adult life. Now? I am of the mind that all of this had to come from someplace. God particle be damned. I still mistrust organized religion. God doesn't need money or my soul. In a way I am going to my house of worship. I guess I am just home-churched.

This day I get to the pulloff just right. Rays of sunlight are starting to shoot past my side of the earth. The railroad tracks were placed by the Rome (New York), Watertown, and Ogdensburg Railroad in 1876. The last train ran on March 31, 1978. Over the years the Hojack—the rail's nickname—has fallen into disrepair. The particular section I hunt will remain nameless. As I get out of the truck I look for human tracks. There are never any. Occasionally snowmobile tracks but the snow cover seems too thin for them today. It will be just like I want. I will be alone for as long as I like. I put on the vest and pack. I load the gun and sling it over my shoulder. I start to walk.

I am keeping my eyes peeled for rabbits. This is not a rabbit-every-ten-feet situation. Sometimes you go a long way before you see one. As you keep looking your eyes begin to sharpen. You wonder how much you missed before you settled in. At first your steps are fast and methodical. *Crunch, crunch, crunch*—each step sounds as if it has been transmitted over a PA system. The air is cold. The temperature was in the teens when I left and isn't any warmer now. In a while my eyes stop watering and my nose stops running. My body is getting used to the cold. My mind, though, it is still cluttered. I am thinking about upcoming business appointments, doctor appointments, tax bills, my parents, my children. We worry about things no other animal worries about. The noise in our heads can be deafening. After an hour my steps are not as fast as before. *Crunch . . . crunch . . . crunch*. My thoughts are lightening, some. I am thinking about if I keep the car a year longer and dine home more maybe I could afford that Purdey shotgun after all.

A couple hours later and the footsteps have lost much of their authority. The sun is shining on my face and I close my eyes. Even with eyes closed the sun is still shining on my face and it feels good. The winter blues are lifting. I walk and look at an old railroad shed. I think of the last guy to work in it. I wonder what his life meant. I wonder if he is still around. I do the math—thirty-six years, it's possible. Then in an instant my reptile brain fires for the first time since the alarm. In a blink of an eye my shotgun finds my shoulder and the report booms through the crisp air. I walk over to the rabbit. He is fat and healthy. His fur is thick and shiny. I put him in the game pouch. I remember how pleased Molly would be to get a fat cottontail like this. I wonder if she taught anyone else the recipe? I tried to tell my daughters about it. They wanted no part of eating rabbit. They love venison but rabbit is on the other side of the line. I still get invited to a few game dinners where it is well loved. Other than that it is for me.

It takes some time for the reptile brain to pull back. It must be about seven miles now. I know a road crosses the tracks at the eight-mile mark. I am hoping to get there and turn around. I like to keep the ditch to my right going and coming. As I hit the road I look at my watch and it tells me it's 1:00 p.m. I know now that I will be back at the truck after dark. I used to do this all in the light. My cheeks and nose are numb and my lungs are engorged. I start walking back, noticing old farmsteads that crawled off a Wyeth work. I am not feeling my legs and I am not really thinking about anything. Layer after layer has lifted. I am, at this moment, free. I am alone, a prophet in my solitude. In our youth solitude terrifies us. We cling to each other like rats on a raft. In our maturity it buoys us.

As the rays of sunlight slip to the other side of the earth, I am happy. I must have picked up the pace some. In the distance, the streetlight I parked my truck under lights up. I am awash in endorphins. I wonder why I don't do this more. It is past shooting light. It will be a one-rabbit day. I don't need more. It is the perfect portion. I might invite a friend and open a Salmon Run Riesling. My legs churn effortlessly and I look out of youthful eyes. Gradually and comfortably, I am enveloped by darkness. It falls like a curtain on a great play. It was a great play. One I will see again. I have been cleansed for now. It will be short-lived. As soon as the ignition fires the engine in the truck, the accumulation will begin again.

If church is a place where a man can go to purify, where he can feel closer to that from which he sprang, then indeed I was in church. Before I turned the key in the ignition I wondered to myself when the next time would be? I could feel the sting in my cheeks as they thawed. Later as I sat under the hot water streaming from the shower head—it felt so good—I could feel the back of my legs pulling. I knew church was starting to be felt by my fifty-year-old body. It was fine, as the aches and pains would remind me of a good day. One of delicious solitude. One that needs to happen often enough to keep us real.

Chapter 9:
Ouananiche

For Ashley

"How cunningly nature hides every wrinkle
of her inconceivable antiquity under roses
and violets and morning dew."
—*Ralph Waldo Emerson*

"Oh, east is east and west is west" . . . is the opening line of Rudyard Kipling's "The Ballad of East and West." The next line, "and never the twain shall meet," defines lines that separate cultures everywhere. Sometimes differences go beyond culture. The geography and the landscape that have evolved over eons can be and are different in different places. I am sure that the landscape helps form the culture. In modern times, the culture has in turn begun reforming the landscape. There are people who feel this is not wise. Then there are some who feel it is the next step in our evolution. I am not sure how much I care. I like to watch and observe but in recent years I have taken as many of my bets off the table as I can. To that end, I spend as much time as I can with my own soul in the outdoors. I was born to filter the cadences of Mother Earth. I work to facilitate that. In order to hear the cadence I find myself going off the beaten path. I have noticed in my time off the path that east is east and west is west.

I am from the East of the United States so I spend my time here. I do love the U.S. West and have made many trips there. The waters and the landscapes of the West seem sharper and crisper than at home in the East; the sky seems bigger and bluer. The landscape of the West is dominated by the Rocky Mountains, which are high and craggy (though not as new as the Canadian Rockies). The Rockies are young, as far as mountain ranges go, and beautiful and dangerous. When I get to the West I understand her call with clarity. It is as the sirens to Odysseus. Every time I fish the West my mind runs through the scenario of coming West. It is a glorious place that has shaped many talented flyfishermen. I can always distinguish where a guy comes from by the way he casts. A Western caster has the most artistic flair. An Eastern caster has a certain economy of motion and accuracy developed for tight conditions.

The Southern fly caster has developed a mixture of both. I am trying to get used to it. I imagine in time and with more exposure, I will. For now it's like watching a cross between a whitetail and a mule deer.

When I think of the East, the one river that epitomizes the region for me is in Quebec. The Caniapiscau River is 458 miles long. Her waters are brooding and moody. She is dangerous but in an understated way. Her currents lie and deceive. Since 1985, the headwaters of the Caniapiscau have been diverted into the La Grande hydroelectric complex. To put that into plain terms, the need for electricity created a reservoir of vast proportions. The Caniapiscau Reservoir is a massive body of water that covers almost 1,700 square miles. Mostly in life, when man screws with things, the law of unintended consequences is harsh. In 1984, when filling the reservoir, officials did manage to drown 9,600 woodland caribou. It never made any news, and really was not significant as it made up about only 1 percent of the George River herd. I am thinking if you were a George River caribou you might feel different.

The real significance of the reservoir is what it has done for the *ouananiche*. A ouananiche is classified as *Salmo salar*. It is said to be the same species as the landlocked salmon of the Northeastern U.S. Recently some biologists have started to notice minute genetic differences but it is a landlocked Atlantic salmon. Ouananiche is French Canadian and may come from the Algonquian. The word's meaning is loosely "He who is everywhere" or "The little lost." In a way, if you have ever fished for them it is fitting. The creation of this big reservoir seems to have increased the average size of the *Salmo salar* living there. The increase, in my experience, has been dramatic. Eight- to twelve-pound fish are rather common. Much bigger ones are more infrequent but not uncommon.

The one difference between saying "landlocked salmon" and "ouananiche" is that it gives people an idea where you're fishing. You mention ouananiche and you are talking about Eastern Canada. It is the natural fish in the East. The fish tend to be sensitive to pressure and pollution. If other species are present, they collectively tend to shrink in size and population. When I hear Western fisherman talk about their cutthroat trout in its rightful place in that landscape, my mind draws an immediate parallel to the landlocked salmon of the East. Both are wild fish that live in wild places. That's one of the things I like best about them. I get to go where the wild things are. It returns me to my childhood. The wonderful book by Maurice Sendak called *Where the Wild Things Are*, written in 1963 (the year I was born), is about a young boy named Max who dons a wolf suit and goes exploring for the wild things. It is a wonderful tale that has stuck with me for many years. The lesson is one of caution about what you expose your young to. I think I keep searching for the wild things because of Sendak.

Of course, getting to the Caniapiscau Reservoir is a challenge: It is by floatplane only. There are several outfitters that service the area and one is as good as another. The accommodations are as simple as the distance and remoteness force them to be. The place I choose has nothing to do with the fishing but rather its dock. It has a very long dock with a large platform at the end. I know it doesn't seem like a big reason to go there but sometimes it does come down to small intangibles.

The trip starts in Wabush, Labrador, Canada. It is a typical northern mining town. I like the people there. They are of tough, northern stock. There is a certain conservation that is present even in their language. They are used to hard, long winters and making the most out of everything. One of the elements I have come to love there is finding fishing flies. I have even resorted to booking my flight a day or two early so that I have time to search. There is an underground brotherhood of salmon fly tiers in the area. I have ended up in some of the strangest places buying some of the strangest flies. The payoff is when you have the one fly that is kicking the living shit out of the fish and nothing else comes close. The downside is, for every fly that delivers, I have hundreds more waiting their turns. In the end it doesn't matter; I love the way salmon flies look. I have always wanted to create presentation or "shadow boxes" with unknown or unnamed flies in them. Maybe when I am in adult diapers and am not much good for anything else other than making shadow boxes, I'll make some. Shitting my pants and making shadow boxes with salmon flies—that's how I'll know I am at the end of the road.

There is a compound in Wabush where the bush planes take off. It has a couple of bars and a restaurant. It caters mostly to fishermen and caribou hunters. I usually come in late July, a little ahead of the hunters. I have caribou hunted there. The place is much less busy in July. Another month and you could use the word "bustle" to describe the activity. In July just a few sports are there. Regardless of when, weather is the schedule-maker. In the far north of the East, Mother Nature is a moody bitch. Clear blue-sky days are rare. On every trip I do recall gathering on the fuel drums by the dock with the rest of the people needing to fly out. It is a natural waiting place, I guess. For hours you sit and wait . . . for something like the clouds to lift here or there. Eventually they do.

When you get in the air you can see that Wabush is just a vicious scar in the wilderness. The giant mining equipment is mind-blowing. It offends your senses, at first. You have to dig deep into your rational mind to understand that this is as it must be. Six going on seven billion people create quite a demand for goods. That has to be sated somehow. Iron ore has to come from somewhere and some of it comes from here. Quickly the scar is behind you and the great wilderness is out in front of you. You gaze upon the whole and unmolested earth. You wonder if it can last. Then you wonder if it can at least last past your existence. I think it can. I know it sounds a bit selfish but it is the best I can do. Eventually there is a tiny break in the wilderness. It is the camp where I will be fishing. I am glad to see it. There will be no electricity, no cell phones, no civilization, and no clocks. Some guys will have watches but I will respectfully ask them to keep the time to themselves. I hate time.

This far north the days are still long. For now the lights stay on well into the evening. The accommodations are not luxurious. There are four rooms with two beds in each. The walls are really just partitions as they do not reach either the floor or the ceiling. I will not share my cubicle because that's how I want it. I will feel the presence of the others in time. Whatever space I can carve out will be a luxury. The bed is small and has a real

Hudson's Bay wool blanket. From past experience I know this is a welcome item. The evenings can be chilling. There is a small "bathroom" next door. Beyond that is a dining tent where we will eat. Past the dining tent is a staff tent. Past the staff tent are thousands of square miles of wilderness. If you fuck up out here it's for keeps.

You get your stuff put up and hurry to rig up a rod and head to the dining tent. It is midafternoon and everyone has decided to take an early dinner and draw straws for guides. It is an informal affair and I find it refreshing. Lately some of the fishing camps/lodges where I have been fishing have held close to military-like preparations. For an old hippie like me that can be far from vacation material. I don't mind an old triangle being beaten like all get out to inform me of the start of the day, but one place I was at had reveille blown at 6:00 a.m. It turned out to be a recording blasted over a set of speakers. (I know some of you are going *reveille*? Isn't it revelry? No it's *reveille* from the French word *reveillez,* which means to wake up. Revelry is something an old hippie like me would gladly wake up to. Yeah, I know the song is wrong. Who cares. Fuck the Boogie Woogie bugle boy.) By way of further mystery, all the amplification speakers on all the poles were permanently disabled one evening. Please note that this is not an acknowledgement to that dastardly deed but rather a brief moment of admiration for that hero, whomever he may be. (Who knows? I might want to return again in the future.)

Dinner is a brief affair. Homemade caribou stew and homemade dinner roles. Everyone is hungry. The food is good. All you hear is the metallic clanking of silverware striking plates. Conversation does not creep in for about fifteen minutes. I guess we spent more time waiting for the floatplane than I thought and used up a lot of our small talk.

The guides come into the dinner tent after a bit. One of them begins to talk. I recognize him from a previous trip. He acknowledges me with a smile. I have done the drawing of the straws before. I had fished with Remi the last time I was there. I did not recognize any of the other three guides. They spend three months in the bush. Some switch camps for a better deal and some just quit. I did well with Remi so I was pulling for him again. Random lots is a hell of a way to assign guides but it's fair. You can bitch, but only about your luck. My luck had me not with Remi but with Richard.

I walked over to Richard. The French Canadian pronunciation is *Reeecharrrdah*. Rolling the second set of r's. I took French in high school and was woefully inadequate during business trips to France. The Quebec dialect makes my poorly spoken French even more remote. Richard was of aboriginal origins. He had the typical black hair and red tones in his skin. It set off the blue in his eyes with the starkest contrast. It was no mystery how he got them. Voyager blood was in all the Eastern Canadian tribes. It creates a fierce and striking look. We did manage to communicate. I said the magic word . . . *ouananiche* and his face lit up with a broad and understanding smile. I walked over to the large square-tailed canoe that Richard had pointed to. I looked her over. She was in good shape. Not all are. It does give clues as to the level of guide I drew.

The Caniapiscau River is deceitful water. It talks in smooth whispers. She lies about everything. The currents can rip with hellacious velocity. She can hide depths of almost one hundred feet and her deceptive calm can turn to pure rage in minutes. A good and wise guide is more essential than a life preserver. Richard appeared to be in his late thirties, small, and wiry. At first glance you would guess much younger but the lines around his eyes gave it away. He had spoken to Remi and knew that I had fished here before. He would not have to "show" me the ropes. The time of day limited the distance and therefore the spots we could fish. We came to a boulder field and began to fish for ouananiche.

The technique they use for the salmon here is a bit different than anywhere else I have fished. You tie a traditional salmon fly—the guides here prefer tandem hooks—on a stout leader. The guides look for a shallow stretch of the river, usually five feet or less. While you are trolling the fly, the guide is scouring the water, looking constantly for salmon beginning to pair up to spawn in a run. Once the guide finds them he positions the boat upstream and backs the boat and fly slowly into the lie. Working it again and again until it solicits a strike or the fish move in annoyance. This is repeated over and over for the bulk of the week.

The salmon have somehow taken on characteristics of both landlocked and anadromous Atlantic salmon. They are indeed stuck in fresh water but do grow way larger than any other landlocked salmon I am aware of. The other quality they have in common with their searun cousins is they appear to lose their appetite when spawning, although not nearly to the extent of ocean fish. On this river they have become a blend of both types. A good day is anything that approaches ten fish. A bad day is— well, I don't have to describe a bad day.

Some people can smile with only their eyes. I could always tell when Richard spotted a nice salmon. The smile on his face would soon follow the rhythmic speeding up and slowing down of the boat. In a way it is like having a fish finder. Which shares the maddening aspect of having one—the knowledge that the fish is there but not interested in eating your fly, or at least what you are trying to sell. Like most things in life it is a numbers game: Get in front of enough fish and it is going to happen.

In a moment when my thoughts began to drift toward other things the first strike happens. Ouananiche can pull you back to reality in a fragment of a second. That first hit, like that first sip of a fine Scotch after an absence, floods it all back. My knuckles get cracked by the spinning reel handle. The blood begins to ooze, reminding me to hang on a little better the next time. I am a bit embarrassed to say that this happens on most ouananiche trips. Seldom does it happen twice in a trip. The lesson is in the throbbing that seems to be in sync with the throbbing of the rod.

Behind the boat the salmon rockets out of the water. It manages a leap with three feet of air underneath. I love all fish but the ones that can fly steal my heart. This marauder is putting on a display of fish in flight. The reel is screaming and I stand to cut the angle of pull. I want to land this first fish. I know I will lose my share this week. Anyone who says they come here and land most of the fish is lying bigger than most fishermen do. Minutes later, the fish is in the net. I hold up three fingers to indicate kilos. This is metric land and they talk in kilos. The guide looks at me to size me up. He is wondering if I am a guy he can be honest with or if he needs to bullshit me to preserve my ego and his tip. I must seem okay because he shakes his head and holds up two fingers. I kind of knew it anyway. I just cannot reconcile the fight with the size. It's like getting beat up by a fifth grader.

That evening we were to take two more salmon of similar size and disposition. I felt the vibe of the place. When I get in tune I can feel the vibe. The place feels old. Ancient. You look around and you venerate it. This is the real "eastness" of the place. As the light gets low you almost see things in the peripheral fields of your vision. Like old ghosts or spirits that dance in the dusk. Some of the natives feel like the place has lots of "medicine" and I do too.

The boat ride to camp brings us past a cross at the point of a nearby island. I had at one time asked about it. It marks a burial site. No one seems to know of whom. The camp owner said it was there before they came. There are some stories that claim it is the grave of a Jesuit missionary. That would make the marker more than two hundred years old. I mentioned that it did look more recent. The camp man, Remi, tells that he and the other guys go to the island and spruce it up before every season. They believe it keeps them safe and prosperous. The only thing for sure is that everyone calls it Dead Man's Point. From past experience I know that the Jesuit rests about five minutes from camp.

The camp comes into view, it is painted a stark white with hot lime-green trim. It is in keeping with the logo of the outfitter. As you draw nearer there is a sign out front with a neatly painted name and logo. Underneath it says "Camp Three." The sign is supported with locally harvested jack pines. Thin but straight, they are painted the electric lime green. Across the bottom of the sign is a second jack pine with large nails sticking out. This is a meat pole in the old tradition. Its main function is for photo opportunities. As we draw nearer I see that the meat pole is indeed being used. As I get out of the boat and close to the sign I get to see the catch much closer. There are five salmon about the size range of those I released. Two northern pike between thirty-five and forty inches. Then there is a big brook trout—I would have to guess it's more than five pounds. I can feel the smile drain off my face.

In old photos from the 1950s and earlier, it is common to see sports standing by the meat pole. Some photos even show hundreds of fish stiff and rigid nailed to the pole. It is proof that these were the ultimate sports. I know the meat served a practical purpose as well. Time has proven that those sports decimated fish stocks everywhere. Here though, it seemed all right. You know that because of the remoteness these deaths would impact very little. That the antique wilderness invited old ways. I also knew that when the salmon were filleted and fried for dinner I would not be shy. The big brookie did offend me a little. I suppose I am programmed more than I like to admit. It is hard country and those who come for the meat as well as the sport are nearer to the place than I am.

Even more to the point, I had killed fish here too. Some for the magical shore lunches. One to get mounted. Yes I have real mounted fish. I like taxidermy. The fish I had mounted was an honest-to-goodness ten-pound ounaniche. One of the sports in camp at the time started giving me the "lecture" about an accurate and lifelike reproduction. I said, "You want me to hang a plastic fish on my wall?"

"It would be an accurate reproduction in every way," he sternly replied.

"Yeah, but *this* is accurate and authentic," I quipped.

"You would rather have a dead thing on your wall than to let him go and have a reproduction to preserve the memory?"

"Well, we do have history." I was now being a dick: "Besides, I can preserve him too. It seems fitting since I prevailed."

I like taxidermy. It is an old art form with so much history in it. You can see very old racks of Irish elk preserved in castles across Europe. In a world where so little is real it gives me comfort. It could be why I like to fish with bamboo rods and flies tied with natural materials. More and more people are living virtual lives. I tend to cling to my real one in defiance. Sometimes the opposite way is too stark. When I was hunting in Africa a herd of elephants came by. One really big bull was covered in pink dots. Pink polka-dotted elephants are usually the realm for the hardcore drunk but I was stone sober. I turned to my professional hunter and asked, "What the hell is that?" Apparently there are now outfitters who sell virtual safaris. You pay lots and lots of money to shoot African game with paintballs. Then it turns out you can have a replica made of the animal you painted. I had to ask if the replica mounts came with the painted exteriors. Somewhere out there is my worst nightmare. A game room with nothing but plastic animals. Even the supposed leather-bound books will be *faux*. Well, come on, leather comes from a cow's ass. At some point things become so bastardized that they border on obscenities. At its core hunting and fishing are blood sports that flow from our days as hunters and gatherers. If you can't handle the concept then buy a tennis racket.

Dinner that night was wonderful. It was just simple meatloaf and gravy with homemade biscuits. Time on the water in the wilderness builds a different hunger. It is more basic and elemental. Comfort food seems to scratch the itch in just the right way. It also leads to a nice nightcap and the sleep can be deep. One of the great things about staying at this camp is that each room comes with a window. I like to sleep cool if I can. If you happen to be in a camp with a fire warden, a cracked window can save the evening. You snuggle with the wool blanket. Your window is cracked just two-fingers wide. I like the sound of the wilderness but it can be very practical if some of the guys in the other room spent the day drinking beer and eating Slim Jims. That night it just felt good—and as my sleep started to come so did the symphony of the wolves.

Sometime that night I went out to relieve myself. In youth you can sleep forever and pee the following Tuesday. Age takes that away. As I stepped out the northern lights were putting on a show. The Aurora Borealis results from a chain of interactions, starting with violent storms on the sun. These solar storms (which increase to a peak in eleven-year cycles) emit charged particles into the solar system. When this solar "wind" collides with Earth's magnetosphere (the area around our planet that is dominated by Earth's magnetic field) some of the particles are captured by Earth's magnetic lines. As more and more of that energy gets caught, it builds up. When it is built up enough the energy discharges. At this point the charged particles rain down into Earth's upper atmosphere. The collision between the charged particles creates the lights. The higher oxygen tends to produce the reds while the lower oxygen adds yellows and green; throw in a little nitrogen for blues.

The technical mumbo aside, it is a beautiful, awe-inspiring show. Many cultures have placed spiritual meaning on the Aurora. Far Eastern cultures believed a child conceived under an Aurora sky would be granted exceptional gifts. Usually a far-north occurrence (or far-south), it sometimes can be seen much farther south in times of extreme solar activity. After the battle of Fredericksburg in the Civil War, the lights could be seen from the battlefield. As it is a very rare occurrence for the Aurora to be seen in Virginia, the Confederate Army took it as a sign that God was on their side. Being a poor portent of military outcomes aside, the light shows are very beautiful.

I mentioned that I favored this place because of the long dock and the platform at the end. This is one of the reasons why. You can go out on the platform at the end of the dock and lay on your back. Looking straight up, you are drawn into the universe, lying on the "altar" with the dancing lights all around you. It makes all your senses tingle. After, you cannot help but feel God is on your side.

The next days are textbook ouananiche fishing in the Caniapiscau River, trolling for salmon in the mornings and evenings, during the day casting the rapids for fast action on smaller salmon and twelve-inch brook trout. In the places you walk you find caribou trails. The George River herd has been migrating through this land for millennia. As you walk down the paths you realize that for thousands of years these trails have been used. These trails could have been walked by other animals, perhaps even Mastodons. You feel the age of Mother Earth here. She hides it well. My mind searches for the Ralph Waldo Emerson quote. It is about how nature in her cunning hides her wrinkles like a vain woman. Even so realizing that not all age is ugly—sometime it's beautiful in its warmth and resilience. Walking along the caribou trail you feel it perfectly. This could be the oldest part of the world and moving west feels younger. East is the side I am on. It is a harder side to hear and feel. As you strain to hear you realize it is soft-spoken and wise. More subtle than today's world allows. The caribou trail moves upward a bit. On one side is some muskeg that looks soft and dry. It is inviting me to sit and relax and soak up the place. I sit and am not disappointed. Richard looks at me, at first in confusion. Then he sits too. We sit and listen and feel the place. No words are spoken, at least not by us.

Eventually, even the poetry must be let go. Time does push and it is a trip for ouananiche and it is time. I just say the word to Richard and he smiles and we walk the old trail back to the boat. I look at my flies and pull out Red Grange. That is what I call it. It is a pattern that has no official name that I know of. It looks like a red Grey Ghost concoction. Red Grange was an old-time college football player. He played halfback and was so tough to stop that his nickname was the "Galloping Ghost." So you can draw the connections and figure out how I came up with the name. Like most trips here, I find the odd fly that just kills. The guide rolled his eyes when I tied it on. They have the blessed flies and any variation from those is met with skepticism. Salmon fishing is old and like all old fishing the traditions can be stifling. Now he motions for me to swing the fly to him. He inspects it well. It has caught four salmon in a little over an hour. Like this story always goes, I have four of these flies to last for four days. This one is hammered pretty good. I know it won't make it. It is okay because that's the thing: It ends up being special.

Much to my surprise, Richard has a special talent. The following morning at breakfast he breaks out a dozen of my Red Grange specials. He stayed up late trying and managing to tie them. The son of a bitch just ruined my market! I wanted to kid him that way. With the language barrier I decided to smile. I am sure he would have understood son of a bitch. But, without the rest of the understanding, you can see how a misunderstanding could arise. By the following day the whole camp was fishing Red Grange and doing great. A part of me wanted to keep the pattern to myself, in some lame way to exert my superiority as a flyfisherman. The bigger part of me was glad to see the camp prosper. The moods were better and fine Scotch flowed.

In fact, on the third day of Red Grange, the mood was so appreciative and happy that I may have caught a buzz on fine whisky. (Single-malt Scotch is always spelled whisky.) The other sports in camp were pouring with light, happy hearts. If a bunch of guys want to catch a buzz hundreds of miles from civilization, why should anyone give a fuck? As the evening wore on my companions started to make moves to go to sleep. I cajoled them to stay and watch the northern lights with me. I made them watch most of the week. They told me they were grateful not to miss such a wonderful display but you can get used to it. I guess I understand. It had been a wild week in the sky and it took a guy like me to want to share the continued light show. As nice as it is to see with other people, watching them alone can be spiritual. I never tire of seeing them.

I lay on my back at the end of the long dock. I wait for the darkness to envelope my persona. As the lights fade and the sky darkens, the sky is so clear. You can feel the heat of the day radiate away. In the unusual clearness the stars twinkle and radiate. Without the light pollution from civilization, the Milky Way just glows like a hot iron fresh from a blacksmith's fire. It is a moonless night but dark would be a wrong adjective. The air is so crisp there is more than a hint of autumn to it. I feel plugged in. The wolves begin to sing. You can hear the joy in their chorus; they feel it too. For some reason the words from a Walt Whitman poem come into my mind. "I sing the body electric"—I feel it, the singing of the body electric. My senses seem to heighten. I am alive. As if on cue the Aurora starts. The sheets and waves of yellow, green, and blue. The wave of the dance of the northern lights. Building in intensity, the red of the color spectrum joins the dance. I am venerable and vulnerable on the altar of the universe. If God isn't here he isn't anywhere. In awe of the sensory overload, my ears pick up a noise. It is a splash in the water. Then another and another. I stand to see the cause. On the water the image of the northern lights is broken up by rings everywhere. As if only for me some sort of feeding frenzy is going on. I quietly grab my rod and tie on a size six Adams. As soon as it hits the water I feel the take and set the hook. It is a good fish. What is it? In moments I land a beautiful and large brook trout. I smile with delight. I slip him and many others back into the colored waters. Each trout I hold, I feel the electric body. In time I feel the need to take a break. I set my rod next to me and lay back and watch the sky once more.

The following morning, I am awakened by the guide Remi. "Did you sleep here all night?" He asks in broken English.

"I must have dozed off," I say and smile.

He sees the rod and the big dry fly and stops for a minute. "Did you see God?"

"I did," I say.

Chapter 10:
The Spot

"And above all, watch with glittering eyes the whole world around you because the greatest secrets are always hidden in the most unlikely places. Those who don't believe in magic will never find it."

—*Roald Dahl*

Welike to believe that we have so much control in our lives. We can see this applied culturally to a people, or solely to individuals. As a people, we sit and work in defiance of nature, who scares us. Her power, when unleashed, can be mind-staggering. I was reading an account of a tragic tsunami and the resulting helplessness and vulnerability offend the human psyche to its core. By way of defense, we work to control nature and short of that we bullshit ourselves into thinking or believing that we are indeed in control. To be honest, if you look wide-eyed you have to admit that any effort to control nature has resulted in pushing more control *away* from us. In some ways, we used to have a semblance of power in the ability to predict certain cycles in nature. I am not sure if we have reached the point where the art of prediction has changed. We seem to carry similar delusions in our personal lives.

In my own personal life, certain events have reminded me of this. I used to have, and now do again, this view that we all are being swept along on a cosmic tide. Forces in the universe push us along. The best we can do is get atop our cosmic surfboards and ride the universal wave. We do not control the direction but we may have some influence over where we ride on the wave, give or take a few feet. Cosmic surfing has a sort of hippie ring to it. I am okay with that. I always thought I had come to a Zen view. I think they—the hippie and the Zen—overlap. Either way, I had to move from a place I really loved to a place I used to live.

I made a list before I put my (former) farm up for sale. "Pros" on one side and "Cons" on the other. It was all bullshit. I knew I had to leave the farm. I was living alone on a farm in a farmhouse that was almost two hundred years old. I was driving two and a half hours each day total for work commitments. I had done it for about twenty-five years. Lately I could not make it home without having to pull over and take a nap. At first I thought it was recovering from the chemo and radiation. That it would get better. After a year it was obvious it wasn't getting better. The upkeep on the farm was getting to be too much. I had to face the fact that life had changed for good. That the cancer had taken its pound of flesh and that was that. Interestingly enough, I have a couple friends who were eager to point out that I was just past my fiftieth birthday and I shouldn't discount that. Friends can be such a mixed blessing.

I often screw up in reverse. I knew it would be just me and Boo. Boo is a fat Devon rex. A Devon rex is a kind of cat. I like cats a lot. I like that you really do not own them. It is a coexistence. Whatever relationship you forge is one that comes about between the two of you and on both your own terms. I love dogs too. Cats forgive when you go away without them. Sometimes they seem to prefer it. There are times I think we do better after a couple days off. I have human friends like that, as well.

So it was my intent to downsize the living situation to accommodate the two of us. Downsizing ended up being a 4,200-square-foot home. I looked at so many smaller homes but I did not like them. I kept coming back to this big house. In the end, I purchased the big house through a short sale. It took several months to navigate the deal and move on it. Then one day you look up and say, "This is my new home." I hate moving so this will probably be my last home.

In a way, it was good being preoccupied with all the transitional crap that accompanies a move. The day of reckoning did arrive. I had not done any outdoor things except for the stuff on trips. In my life most of my days afield take place near home. Is there really any other way? Here I was, with nowhere to go. The proverbial fish out of water. I used to live near this new house many years ago. The area has changed so much. I made a few quick visits to some of the old places. It was sobering to know that I was going to have to start over again. When I moved to the farm twenty-five years ago, it was fun to explore and learn. I was not sure if it would be the same. It is one of the big changes as we age. We are not as eager to restart. Some of it is purely that you wonder if you can cut it. The rest is resentment that all the dues you paid were in an account that's now closed. Silly thinking but very human.

The problem with being fifty and starting over is all about comfort. You spend so long building a comfort zone that venturing outside of it is difficult, forget about losing it. I sat and thought about it. I remember being young and just approaching life as a series of adventures. One of the things about moving is you come across shit you forgot you had, shit you are embarrassed you have, shit you are thankful you didn't lose but thought you did, and mostly just plain old shit. In the pile of shit I forgot I had was a box of old county roadmaps. They were the counties surrounding where I went to college and were not immediately useful. What was useful was that when I looked at the maps, I could see where I had placed neat little Xs next to pieces of water. Sometimes I had written a word like "brown." I knew that meant brown trout.

In pouring over the maps, I began to understand the young man who wrote these notations. The earlier version of me. There was method to what I had done. I valued the method enough to put the maps away in a shoebox. Here, two and a half decades later, the method had finally come to light again. I was finding meaning how in a way I had no possible idea of knowing I would all those years ago. I am sure I thought I would want to fish those areas again and the maps would help. (I have kept them handy. I can see making a trip there. I would not want to disappoint my youthful self.) The unintended value is the methodology. It showed me how to approach a new area in a way that worked for me. Contemplating it all comes with a bit of weirdness. It is very much like having a time capsule and going back in time to talk to yourself to solve a current problem. It is the kind of cool, quirky, sci-fi feel I like.

I began to find fishing places again. In the way I used to. It was coming back. I must admit that having the Internet is a great boon. In a short time I have been able to find a few places. Some good public fishing is now where it was not. I like that. I often bemoan that my sport has undergone some ugly changes but it has seen some good ones too. There is a bit of water at the Caledonia Fish Hatchery that I enjoy. The fish hatchery at Caledonia, New York, is the oldest hatchery in the Western Hemisphere. It was started in 1864 by Seth Green. If you don't know that name you should. He was the father of modern aquaculture. Some even give him credit for inventing the fishing reel. We do know for sure he planted ten thousand American shad in the Sacramento River in 1871. You can be sure that at one point in your life, a trout you have caught has a link to the Caledonia hatchery.

I have always liked connections. How the things we do touch the other things we do. The fabric of our lives is knitted delicately with some sort of pattern. Sometimes you have to stand back quite a ways to see the pattern but it is there. I guess that this nice little spring creek next to the hatchery is no accident. That this spot for the hatchery was chosen for its supply of cool, clean water. The creek immediately adjacent to the hatchery is for flyfishermen with all the usual regulations. If you are thinking it must be easy fishing because it is right next to the hatchery, then you would be wrong. In fact, the fish there are educated and on some days quite maddening. It turns out many of the fish there are wild. Makes you wonder about stocking survival rates. There are always people fishing here. It is all right with me as I have never had a problem with anyone. I always look at fly fishing as an East versus West proposition. I think Western fisherman are used to so much more room. It makes it a different game. I am an Eastern guy so I am all right with an angler and a rod thirty or forty feet away. Sometimes it makes for a pleasant afternoon.

I have a habit of showing up there around 3:00 p.m. I like to take off a little early from work. I like to fish the evening hatches if they come off. If not I suffer through casting a freshwater-shrimp pattern. This day I came to my spot. I like to call it my spot but more accurately it is my favorite spot on this stream. On this day a young man was in my favorite spot. There was a time that something like this would have put me off. Now, I just sat on a rock and watched. He looked to be in his mid-twenties. His equipment was modest. I was glad of that. I hate watching some kid who looks like he stepped out of an Orvis catalog. His casting was good and I enjoyed watching him. A few times, he glanced over his shoulder at me. I didn't intend to make him nervous. There was a smaller pool a few yards downstream. I walked in and began fishing. As I started to cast I noticed a sulfur hatch starting to come off. The sulfur hatch here can be very good but the bugs tend to be small. I tied on a size eighteen sulfur pattern with the help of glasses I now have to carry. I call them my "fly glasses" because I use them to tie on smallish flies. I used to be able to do it with naked eyeballs. When the guy at the fly shop wants to sell me something smaller than a size twenty-two, I just look at him.

"You need some size twenty-six Disco Midges," he'll say.

Yeah? I need fish that aren't so fucking special! I can't even see the fly; how the hell can I see the hook eye? The guy at the fly shop is showing me the detail with a fifteen-power magnifying glass. All I can think about is who is tying these and how long has it been since he got laid?

The problem with a very good hatch is you simply have too many choices. The fish are eating but you can get lost in the volume. Although it still is nice to be in the middle of a hatch.

I am picking up a few fish. Mostly rainbows with a few wily fat browns mixed in. I look up at the kid. He is in the middle of my spot, there are fish rising all around him, and he is not hooking anything. This is always a tough moment. Do you say anything? It is always great to be helpful but most of us take to the rod because we didn't want to take to the bottle or any other thing to escape. I started to watch him again. He had tied on a sulfur pattern but it was way too big. I knew he had no shot and the hatch would wind down in a while. I took out one of my flies and walked over to him and said, "Put this on. It will make a big difference." He did and it did. Dusk was getting on as I waded out. He was still casting so I sat on the rock and watched him catch a couple more trout.

He waded out and sat on the rock next to mine. "Do you want your fly back?'

"No, you keep it," I said. "You did good."

"Thank you. I didn't have anything that small."

The conversation went on for a bit. It was the usual cordial fisherman banter. Polite and steeped in tradition. Then it turned as often it does to fishing spots. The young man wanted to show the old guy he knew some things. I liked that. Then he mentioned something that shot right up my back. That he had been catching fish in a place that I knew years ago held trout. Then development and pollution turned the stream into a slow and dirty affair. He told me that the state and some other groups reclaimed the stream. That trout were in it and growing again and although the area was somewhat crowded, it was well stocked and easily fished. Way easier than this. It wasn't the news of this stream that had my brain spinning. It was water that this water touched. It was a pocket tucked in the middle of plain sight that no one knew about. At least that's the way it use to be. If the trout were here they had to be there? Right?

I went to bed that night jazzed up. That kid had no idea what he started. Years earlier, when I was in my teens, I lived in these apartments. Behind these apartments was a valley and this stream ran through it. It was a wild pocket that had been developed all around. Hills came up on both sides and were heavily wooded. It was a beautiful stream and it ran maybe three quarters of a mile. I would set up a tent by its banks. There was even a pool that was a good eight feet deep. I would bathe and swim there. I camped there for weeks at a time and never saw another soul. Now some kid has told me that a stream that connects to this a mere two miles away is loaded with fat trout. It was one of those ideas that just keeps kicking around until it grows into a kind of obsession. I knew I would have to get back there and fish it. I wondered how much had changed in more than thirty years. I decided a weekday would be the best. I got on the Internet and used Google Earth. The spot was still there. Nothing had been developed. I sort of knew it would be like that. I wondered if it was a declared wetland and maybe that was why?

I drove to where my old apartment complex was. The good news was that the apartments were now senior-citizen housing. God bless those Boomers. I could park right against the hill. It was too steep for a walker to get up. I looked along the length of the back parking lot and saw nothing but game trails. I was encouraged. I checked the weather forecast and Wednesday looked clear and cool. It would be the day. I decided to fish a seven-foot, 4-weight bamboo rod with a Peerless reel. I also decided to bring a pack. I knew there would be only five or six good spots to fish but I would fish them slow. I would bring a coffee pot and make some cowboy coffee to go with some sandwiches and some good cheese and baguettes. Good or bad it would be a day to see. To hide in plain sight. That appealed to me.

We have a grocery store in Western New York named Wegmans. They are a growing chain whose stock-in-trade is based on a stellar-produce concept. They provide unbelievable range and freshness of produce and charge top dollar for it. Turns out people will pay for the good goods. Not far from my home is their flagship store. They carry decadence to the extreme in the food department. You can purchase truffles for more than the cost of an ounce of gold, go twenty yards and buy an equally extraordinary expensive amount of beluga caviar. I often walk through this store slack jawed hoping some rich family will want to adopt a semi-worn-out, fat trout bum. If for no other reason, simply because no other rich family has one. They could talk about where I was fishing and how much it cost them. How it was worth it to sponsor me because it was so Zen and rare. I know I won't be eating caviar on my day. I am here to make sure

I get the right stuff for my day. Over the course of the years you learn that you can create a good day. That catching fish will push it over the top. Without the fish, if done correctly, it's still a good day. That's why I'm at Wegmans.

In the fruit section, I stumble across round Oriental pears. I buy two—one to test at home, and one if it works out. I come across some honey crisp apples. I used to be an apple farmer, I know my apples. I buy two anyway. I stumble over to the coffee aisle. This place is so haute couture that I never feel comfortable here. I probably blend in on the outside but my soul is on fire. It could be the price—$15.99 a pound—for the coffee. I know I will pay it but I also know it will bother me for a bit. Now I am stuck. On the one hand, there is this Blue Mountain Kona Hawaiian and on the other is this Costa Rican Thunder Fuck something or other. In the end, I commit the ultimate sin: I mix a half pound of each. I grind the beans coarse. There is an older woman watching me, with a rock on her finger the size of my eye. Her lower lip is sticking out in disgust. She screwed up, she let me know it bothered her. So I mix a half pound of espresso with decaf. She just shakes her head and walks away. I know I will never use it. I just pissed away sixteen bucks. It was worth it. I go to the bakery and grab a rosemary garlic loaf of bread. I pick out a nice *sopresatta* salami from about thirty-two choices. I get to the *fromage* department—in another store it would be the cheese section. They are giving samples of some soft goat-milk cranberry brie cheese. It's so good, I buy half a pound. On the way out the door there is a bin for some halfway house. I put the messed-up coffee in it. Three steps later the Catholic guilt that haunts my life has me putting the apples in too. I hope the pears are as good as they look.

Tuesday night comes. I pack the backpack carefully. I even put in some nicely split pieces of hickory. I wonder if the fire pit I built in my teens is still there. I make two sandwiches with the *sopressata* and mustard. I put the pears in a small Tupperware and the cheese in another. I dig out my old coffee pot. I look at it as I hold it. It has been a few years since I have used it. I really don't drink much coffee anymore. The exception being Dunkin' Donuts iced coffee, extra cream no sugar. I used to lug that pot all over. Everyone makes cowboy coffee a little different. I put water in, and then three or four giant heaping tablespoons of coffee, and then crack an egg without breaking it, and then boil the hell out of it. I let it calm down. Cream and sugar help if it is not very cold out.

I picked the short fly rod because I just could not know if the foliage had closed in over the stream. If I had to work close then the short stick would be handy. I put together a nice book of flies. The selection was the kind anyone would put together to probe an unknown situation. I knew I wanted a long lunch. I wanted to stretch out the day. The best way to do this was to bring a book. I was starting to be my anal self. Debating what book to bring. I grabbed three paperbacks—*Atlantic Salmon* by Lee Wulff, *Even Brook Trout Get the Blues* by John Gierach, and *A Fine and Pleasant Misery* by Patrick F. McManus. I was done. Now if I could find sleep. I never can the night before fishing. As a young boy waiting for my father to pick me up for one of several fishing trip each summer, I can remember sleepless nights. The alarm would be set for 4:30 a.m. It would not matter that I could not sleep. I would watch as each number flipped. It was so strange. The clock had twenty-four hour paddles that would flip and sixty-minute paddles that would flip. Each paddle had numbers printed on them to look like LED displays. A fake LED display, and I watched each paddle turn in excruciatingly slow progression. Thank God I now have a real LED display.

The morning comes. I don't know if I slept or not. I leave the TV on now when I have trips coming up. I find it helps me drift off. The only problem is I wake up wanting to buy something I don't need. It must be the strategy of those infomercials: to pound you in a semiconscious state. If you were fully awake you would change the channel. It's the only reason I can think of why I have watermelon-scented thigh cream.

I live close enough to my spot. I can get there from my driveway in about fifteen minutes. I pull into the back lot of the senior condos. It is very quiet as I grab my pack and rod case. It is a two-piece rod so the case is small and not conspicuous. I start up the bank and up the hill. I remember shooting right up that hill as a fifteen-year-old boy. *Shooting* is not the verb I would use now. The son of a bitch is steep. I want to get up it quick and get out of sight. What good is a secret spot if people know about it? I get up it and over the top in about fifteen minutes. I have to sit and let the burn fade. It gives me a chance to look down the hill anyway. It is mid-September and the leaves are starting to turn. I can see the stream. It looks like it did all those years ago. The only difference is the woods are a bit more mature. The understory has died off. I can see a doe and a fawn just out of his spots near the bottom. I see trillium near the far bank. Thousands of people move around within a quarter-mile of this place every day. A mile and a half downstream, this river passes under a major highway. The sun is up enough to be in my eyes. I start down to the water.

I decide to fish the water methodically. I will walk to one end and fish it to the other. If I go slow I will get to my "camping" spot close enough to noon to take a break. The end I decided to start at is bounded by a private road for a paving company. As I walk there I look at the place with a different eye. As a boy it was a place away from adults. A place to kiss a girl, to drink some Mad Dog 20/20 with friends, to smoke whatever. Growing up under the specter of the bomb was peculiar. It was just after the 1960s. People were reeling from Vietnam. Mothers were just starting to get mad(d). Ronald Reagan's approach to peace was to build more nukes. This was a place to get away. I saw cottontail rabbits. Whitetail deer. There were crayfish shells scattered about the banks, so there were raccoons. I saw cardinals, sparrows, blue jays, and various songbirds. The flora was varied— some wondrous mature red and white oaks and maples, spruces and firs and pines. I am not going to write a detailed list here but I have started one for myself. We always like to think of life as delicate and precious and in some ways it is. In other ways it is tough and tenacious.

I remember years ago coming across a principle called the Gaia principle, or hypothesis as some call it. To oversimplify, it basically states that the earth is a self-regulating complex system. Gaia evolves through a cybernetic feedback system that organisms co-evolve with their environment. In a way I can see it happening here. Life filled up the available space the best it could. I like that. We want to think that nature needs us to survive. She doesn't, we need her. I wonder if she decides to keep us?

Here we are. The first fishy-looking place. When I was young I did try to fish the place. It had its problems. I remember catching a few sunfish. That was it. I looked into the water. It looked different. It ran a bit quicker than I remembered. This pool appeared to be four or five feet at its greatest depth. I tied on a Stimulator pattern. I've always found them to be a good searching fly. It was an orange-headed fly with a yellow body and a white elk wing. The overall fly had brown dry-fly hackle with orange dubbing. It was a size twelve. I tested the knot and then I cast to the head of the pool. I did not even have a chance to mend my line. A vicious strike and a quick hook set followed. Minutes later, I had in my hand a pretty sixteen-inch rainbow. Fish generally have three looks. One is well-proportioned, in which the fish is in three proportionate parts. The head, body, and tail all are about a third and it is so handsome. One is either an old fish or undernourished. The head appears to be the largest part: a triangle with the head being the large base. This often happens in overpopulated waters. The last is where the fish looks like a football—the head appears too small; the section between the head and tail is a rotund football shape. It occurs where food is ample and the fish pig out. This trout was that last kind, with a bright red stripe all the way down its thick slab sides. I was tickled pink.

I had taken my time and fished that hole slow and sure. Three more bright rainbow trout came from that place. I lost two others. One rolled on my fly that I was sure went better than twenty inches. It's always like that. That's the hook—the gimmick the fishing gods use to keep us well entrenched in the game. I moved up to the next hole. I was fishing slow. Savoring each bit. My footprints were the only ones I saw. I was enraptured. This one fished just like the one before. My Stimulator had to be replaced. I tied on a new one. I did fill up a flask with some fine single-malt Scotch. I took a break and a sip of twenty-one-year-old Scotch. The sun was breaking through the mature treetops. It was cool and crisp. I reached into my pack and drew out one of the pears. I took a bite and the juice ran down my chin. It mixed with the fruity finish of the Scotch so well. I could feel the smile on my face. Life, at this moment, was delicious.

Finally, I came to the deep hole that I used to camp next to. It's funny to come back to a place you've spent some time at. In a way you can feel the old ghosts. The pieces of yourself you left behind. I believe we always leave bits of ourselves. In that way, our energy inhabits a place. Most places are neutral and some are good and some not so good. I was once in the London Tower. I don't care to ever go back. I liked the old vibes I laid down at this fishing and camping spot. The question at hand was should I fish this hole before lunch or after? I decided to fish it before lunch. I fished it with a methodical approach. I expected that this would be good. I thought its depth would have some significance. Things don't always work out the way you hope. The pool yielded one sixteen-inch rainbow. They seemed to be cookie cutter. How can you complain when the cookies are fat, beautiful rainbow trout? Not me, not ever.

I came to the spot I used to camp on. It looked as if no one had been there since. The fire circle I made was untouched. I needed to pull a few plants and reset one of the logs to sit on. In a short while, I had a small fire going. I was glad to unload the wood from my pack. I would not need to bring any again. It would take some time to burn up the deadfall at the camp area. I just sat there looking around. Off to the right was a pile of Mad Dog 20/20 bottles. I would take them out a few at a time. It was ironic that I came back to clean up my campground. That had significance on a bunch of different levels. Just past the bottles there was a tree with JH + LL carved on it. I laughed out loud. I hadn't thought about LL in thirty years. I enjoyed my coffee. My lunch was so good. I decided to read for a long while. I wanted to come out the other end at dusk so I could sneak out. This was my place. Somehow it always was. It reminded me of a Roald Dahl quote: "And above all, watch with glittering eyes the whole world around you because the greatest secrets are hidden in the most unlikely places. Those who don't believe in magic will never find it."

I must believe in magic. I prepared to find this place. I know what a find this is. I also know it could go at any time. In reality, it turns out to be six holes with a couple of smaller fishing spots. That it could be ruined by only two or three of the wrong people. I won't ever say anything to anyone.

It turns out, the best pool was two after the camp pool. To be more accurate, it was the fifth pool. I spent well over an hour there. It delivered the fat rainbows one after another. There would be a surprise for me. From that pool came an eighteen-inch brown trout. I was so delighted. I realized this was the kind of spot that came along once in a lifetime. If that. I thought swearing the kid to a solemn oath and sharing it with him. Well, I thought about it for the briefest of moments. Then a thundering sentiment bellowed, "Fuck him." So that's how it stands today. I go there casually. It remains untouched. I always pack a nice lunch as part of the ritual. I hope it lasts. All I can do is what I am doing. I am good with that.

Chapter 11:
Grasshoppers in Chile

"What is the difference between you and
a cricket?"
    —*Nick Adams in "Big Two-Hearted River"*
    by Ernest Hemingway

PART I

There is a fly shop in Redding, California, through which I've booked high-end fly-fishing trips. Conveniently, it's called The Fly Shop. Before I found them I used to go the sportsmen's shows and book the trips myself. I would walk from booth to booth looking at the scrapbooks full of photos and listening to some of the best and most-polished sales pitches on the planet—and often part with more money than I could afford. I had this sense of urgency about going to fabled fishing places.

My sport, fly fishing, was changing all around me. It was becoming mainstream and guys with big money were coming in and pricing out the regular guys like me. I guess it was a lot like the housing market in the West when the exodus from Los

Angeles began. People wanting to escape L.A. sold their homes for very high prices and went looking, mostly north, where they encountered much cheaper property. Bidding wars often ensued with properties selling for many thousands of dollars higher than the asking prices. Property values exploded. Great thing, right? Not if you were a native Californian and you suddenly couldn't afford to live in your hometown. You were full of anger and resentment, and if you could you tried to figure out another option.

In my case, and in the case of the people like me who were active flyfishers when the sport was a fringe affair, we saw the tidal wave coming, the sport was changing, and it looked like maybe this was for keeps. We wanted to get ahead of the curve a little and get our kicks before we couldn't anymore. We spent money we didn't have to fish places before the crowds descended; many places we didn't get to fish.

Along the way, I got fucked pretty good by those opportunists with dollar signs in their eyes. My biggest mistake was trying to navigate who was honest and who wasn't at the shows and in the advertising in the back of magazines. It didn't take long to find out that the bad outweighed the good—greatly. In a twisty turn of events, I ended up getting to know a guy named Pat at The Fly Shop in Redding, California. He always put me on good trips. Let me clarify: He always put me on trips where the fishing was special. There were times I found myself in the "Orvis" culture so deep I began to itch. I am not sure if that is avoidable, anymore. The one thing I can say is that using professional outfitters to fish new places, which usually goes against my freewheeling ways, is one of the smarter things I have done.

February is a miserable time of year where I live in Central New York. The hunting is done. It is so cold. The snow that I don't mind in December is now dirty and oppressive. How many times can you clean your firearms and sort your fishing equipment? The days are short and the nights are long. Too much time in front of a computer screen can be troublesome. It is so easy to click "Confirm the bid." You watch the time wind down on the eBay auction site and realize you will be getting yet another bamboo rod. Then you wonder if you might need a reel to match it. In the deepest part of your psyche you know that in the thirty—or is it forty?—4-weight reels you own there should be one that fits the Payne you just purchased. There is a queasy feeling that this may even cause budgetary anomalies. Luckily, February is short. This compulsive impulsive shopping is a flyfisherman's prayer for spring to arrive.

The prayers may have worked, in a way. Checking email, you get one from your friend, Pat. He has a deal for you. Some guy (it's always *some guy)* had to cancel a great trip to the Grasshopper Lodge in southern Chile. If I could leave in ten days, the trip would be greatly discounted, Pat writes. Even with the great discount, the trip is expensive. I have looked at the trip in The Fly Shop's catalog over the years with a covetous heart. Each pondering and pouring-over always ended when the price came into view. I sat in front of the screen looking at the new price. In my head I knew that my oppressive winter had its inverse season in the other hemisphere. In another compulsive impulsive moment I sent the response back to Pat: OK! Trying not to think about the budgetary impact, I focused on how to get the Payne rod in time. You have to have priorities—no matter how fucked up other people might think those priorities are.

The trip to the Chilean Patagonian region is more than five thousand miles away from my cold New York home. You always call to ask what you need to bring. Sure, the list of clothing is nice but it is the flies I want to know about. I was told this was terrestrial heaven—so bring hoppers. Dave Whitlock has even fished the place and you can buy hoppers from him, I was told.

The second most famous hopper in fly fishing is Dave's. (The first were the ones used by Nick Adams. Sorry, Dave, Hemingway was that good.) Then you go about rooting out all the "off-brand" terrestrials you can find. The shopping for the flies is crazy. If you are a dry-fly guy, you buy the odd terrestrial in smaller quantities because it is a niche fly. It has to be a confluence of events to fish them—sometimes hard, sometimes easy. In the summer months, you always keep a few on you. It is like the secret prayer of all dry-flyfishermen. It is the whisper in Hemingway's *Big Two-Hearted River.*

The thought of going to a place where for two months of the year big brown trout eat mostly large grasshoppers kept me sleepless. For several days, Express Mail packages arrived and I pried them open with greedy fingers. I extricated and aligned flies with precision according to size and type in my meticulously arranged fly books. The pile of fly books by the door slowly grew—next, they would have to be redone.

Flying to another continent with fishing gear is a gut-wrenching task. You are torn between wanting to take what you love and fearing losing what you love. What you put on an airplane isn't necessarily what you take off the plane. In the end, with creative engineering and duct tape, I carried on the rods, reels, and flies. The rest was minutia.

When you fly to Chile, most international flights land in the capital, Santiago. In the last-minute dance of the cancellation (and therefore discounted trip), the time between my flight into Santiago and my subsequent flight to Coyhaique was tight. To complicate matters, the flights were on different (and domestic) airlines, so I had to pay a special entry tax, and I really speak no Spanish.

Coming through the long tax line, I must have looked the part of the panicked tourist. A young man came to me and asked how he could help. I remember thinking, "Holy shit . . . English!" I showed him my boarding pass. It was less than a half hour to the boarding time. He told me not to worry, that for twenty dollars he would help me make it. I thought, "Fuck, I would give you way more not to miss this flight!" I dug into my pocket and handed him a crisp twenty-dollar bill. I told him if I made the gate in time he could have another. He motioned with his hand and from the crowd a couple of his friends came and grabbed my bags. In minutes I was at the counter. I checked in. Then he escorted me to the gate just as they were to allow boarding. He delivered on his promise and I handed him another twenty.

The flight from Santiago to Coyhaique was much shorter than the previous flight from Chicago to Santiago. The exhaustive effects of flying are cumulative. I was getting pretty crunchy by the time the plane landed.

The airport in Coyhaique is small. A small, metal roll-down door is lifted and your luggage is placed through the door. This is the extent of baggage claim. I looked around and did not see anyone who resembled the people who were supposed to be picking me up. There was an American-looking fellow so I went up and asked, "Are you with the Grasshopper Lodge?" He looked at me and answered, "No." We conversed and it turned out he was from Ohio somewhere. He was down here starting up a competing business. He knew the folks from the Grasshopper Lodge. He said they were not on the best of terms but he would call them for me.

He came back from his car. He told me they weren't expecting me until the next day. They would be by to get me but it would be several hours. I frowned. I was tired and just wanted to be somewhere I was supposed to be. He must have sensed my consternation. He told me he was waiting to pick up one of his clients and we could pass the time together. The Coyhaique airport is small and with a rather quick once-over you see the whole place. As fishermen do, we could always talk about fishing. If gear is nearby, the conversation always moves to "show me what you got." There must be something about a fly rod being assembled: All the sports in the tiny airport started to draw near. It was an odd experience because the only people in the airport at that moment were sports. For one reason or another, we were all waiting to catch trout in the southern part of South America. Eventually five or six guys were assembling and comparing rods. I know . . . but sometimes a cigar is just a cigar.

When we got to flies, it got a little weird. As I unzipped fly book after fly book, jaws went slack. I was swelling with pride. When the "holy fucks" started you would have thought I (not Al Gore) invented the Internet. I was just amazed and proud that my fly collection was being appreciated for the masterpiece it was.

"How the hell did you get that?" one gentleman said and stared in amazement. I replied that I was an aficionado and the Whitlocks were authentic. "No," said another. "How did you get them *here*?" I was now a bit confused. "I carried them. What do you mean?" It was explained to me: They all had their flies confiscated at customs due to a "bird flu" outbreak. One guy showed me a handful of rubber spiders. He had to beg to get them in. Customs, I thought? The intellectual light slowly began to brighten. I had been escorted around customs for twenty dollars! By this time, the light had illuminated enough for me to tell a nice white lie. "They just didn't seem interested in them. Didn't even ask to look." Both statements were true. The lie was in the omission.

It turns out that if you have a full assortment of flies in the Coyhaique airport when there is a bird-flu outbreak, you have some unforeseen opportunities. I was offered ridiculous money for some of the flies. I told the gentlemen I could not ethically sell them at a tremendous profit. That I would give a couple to each. The old fishing code demanded that I do that. To take ten dollars for a fly I spent only one on would have serious repercussions in the karmic scheme of things. If there is a place where karma has a heavy hand, it is in fly fishing. I figured out what I could comfortably spare and divided them up. The other sports were grateful in an insatiate way.

I determined that selling the flies would indeed be bad juju but trading was okay. In the end, I got a pretty Abel reel, a fine graphite Winston 5-weight, and a twenty-two-year-old bottle of Scotch. I wished I could have traded more but I needed to have enough of a fly inventory to be sure for myself. In my life I have done some strange things. Smuggling contraband flies into Chile and turning wonderful gains through trade in the Coyhaique airport is up there. Somehow the fishing gods were smiling on me. You just know the experience is going to be great.

Eventually the ride I needed showed up. I loaded all my stuff and was taken to a nice house and given a nice room. Checking over my paperwork, I saw that I was indeed a day early. I felt lucky that the lodge saw fit to pick me up. It would have been easy to say, "We just can't help you right now."

Apart from the room, I was really on my own. I didn't mind that a bit. It gave me a chance to look around. The gypsy in my soul relishes such chances. I did manage to find a small outdoor market. The town square had an old-world charm. It was reminiscent of the famous final scene in *Butch Cassidy and the Sundance Kid*—the town square, where you could imagine an execution by firing squad. Brutal and romantic all at once. I was compelled to see if there were any bullet holes. Then I remembered Pinochet ruled not long before and I just might find bullet holes and they would not be fictional ones of the Wild West banditos in the dime-store novel, but the real ones of oppressive dictators.

I wanted to find food. You can be on the go for so long that the thought of food eludes you. Eventually biology will let you know. I found a quaint little restaurant. It had a great menu and I pored over it. I ordered a beer, which came ice cold, and I ordered a salad with chicken. A few other people were there. A beer or two later I had a giant plate brought out to me. Upon it was not a salad but a huge chunk of fire-roasted meat. I looked around and it was the same meal on each plate. I tried to tell the gentle lady that I ordered the salad. She just looked at me with uncomprehending eyes. Suddenly a patron from another table tried to help. "Carne asada," he said. After a few moments when language was a struggle I figured out that you get what you get. Tonight was big chunks of roasted beef. The smell had reached my hunger and that was it. Some say hunger is the best sauce, but this meat was delicious. A last meal on death row was never relished like this. I know Americans are picky about their beef, but Chilean beef meets any mark anywhere.

The next morning, the guests who were not flying by the seat of their pants arrived. In a few hours we would be taking the long trip south to the lodge. The big van was loaded up with passengers and equipment. As each hour passed, the road became narrower and windier. In spots, the edge that the van hugged was bounded by a steep and foreboding cliff. Vertigo came often. For the last few hours, I kept my eyes trained at my feet. Looking over the edges of precipices has always messed with me. I could never have been a roofer. Eventually the road turned terrible and, at just the right moment, after we split up a rather large herd of alpacas, the lodge came into view.

The lodge was a compound, of sorts. It really lacked any typical character. In North America, lodges have a certain look. There are several varieties that usually match up with the area in which they are located. This was a compound with peculiar but pleasant architecture. There were pretty guest chalets scattered about the campus. There was one main building that was the main lodge. You could hear the other guests talking. This was also an enormous ranch. Horses and alpacas were the other businesses. It was apparently a massive ranch even by Western U.S. standards. It was mentioned that the proprietor was a nephew of none other than Augusto Pinochet, that these lands were procured for the nephew.

People are complex and have many loves. The compilation of our loves makes us who we are. We draw all our interests together and combine them through our one filter, our soul. One of my other loves is history. I love the story of humanity. How we came to be who we are. Man has evolved physically, slowly over millennia. We have, metaphysically, evolved at a breakneck pace over the last ten thousand years. I find this history intriguing. Along that timeline great people have come. People who have edified humanity and left enduring values. When I think of Martin Luther King, I feel that. Unfortunately, there have been some bad players on the timeline. Augusto Pinochet was a bad man. He was a dictator propped up by bad American political agendas. A dictator who caused thousands of people to vanish in the night. As I looked across the compound, I could see the family resemblance in the nephew and it chilled my blood. As I was introduced and shook his hand, my mind started working through history. I knew my prejudice had nothing to do with him. We cannot chose our family tree and every tree is capable of producing one bad apple. I was beginning to reason away my moral vertigo. I was here for a fishing trip. So I hurried the welcoming and whisked off to my chalet. I was staying in a pretty fishing chalet under the peaks of the Andes Mountains, the valued guest of Augusto Pinochet's nephew. Life can be wonderfully, eclectically strange. That part I like.

PART II

Where Did All the Grasshoppers Go?

Many of the guides working at the lodge were American guides. It was a good situation for them. The opposing seasons in our hemispheres made it possible for some of the young men to guide year 'round. We'll call my guide Bob to protect him from the incriminating things we did.

Bob guided the fine blue-ribbon trout streams of the American West. We chatted and had friends in common. It is often that way in our sport. There are a limited number of circles and unless you are a total prick or a recluse you eventually have contact with a bunch of these people. Talking about who you know is often a way to legitimize your pedigree. It's name-dropping plain and simple but it serves another purpose. It's like knowing the secret handshake so your guide can at least understand you have some fish sense. It saves you both time and helps to develop an understanding of expectations.

After we shared some stories about people we had in common, Bob felt he had to tell me something. Looking at his boots with his hands in his pockets, the kind of body language that says, "It ain't my fault but . . ."

I looked at him and said, "Hey man, no worries, it is what it is and we'll figure it out." I was fully expecting to be told that they paired me up with someone I didn't know. That can be a regular nightmare. I had paid extra for one-on-one guide service just to avoid such a disaster. The bombshell was a sharp left-hand turn from what I was expecting.

"There ain't no grasshoppers," he said.

"What do you mean . . . there ain't no grasshoppers?" I said, trying to get my head around the thing.

"Well, for some strange reason, we have not seen them. Not sure if we will this season."

My mind started to flash in different directions. I wanted to bang my head on the ground. "What flies to fish if there are no grasshoppers?" was the only question I didn't ask before the trip. You just figure that there would be grasshoppers at the world-famous Grasshopper Lodge. Bob spoke on cue—he had done this before, the poor bastard. "I think I got a few alternatives figured out," he said. He was doing the best he could. It was obvious this was a bad problem and everyone was coping. He helped me unpack my stuff and string up a few rods. It was agreed that we would skip the evening session and hit it in the morning. I was tired so sleep—deep sleep—was a good option.

The morning came fast. My alarm clock was persistent enough to stir me awake. Sometimes a good sleep can bring fresh perspective. I looked around my chalet and realized it was beautiful. I could smell the wonderful aroma of fresh coffee. As I followed my nose to the breezeway I could see that a fresh pot, along with some fresh fruit and cheese, had magically appeared. I sat drinking coffee and nibbling on the food. I like getting pampered. I think it is a nice feeling, once in a while.

There was a knock on my door—a very slight rap. I went to the door and one of the caretakers asked me if I was coming to breakfast. I was confused. After a short conversation, it seemed the coffee and fruit and cheese were a warm-up to breakfast. I ambled over to the lodge. Breakfast was a beautiful affair complete with the red-stag mount that made you stare. The table was massive oak and very old and ornate. It had the look of old European royalty. I was late. I noticed that after I noticed everything else. My seat, next to Pinochet, was waiting. I sat and softly apologized for my tardiness. Courses of food hung on the table. It was obvious that decadence was the order of the day. I just sat there and soaked it all in. In my quest to fish places before I could not, I was getting used to being in over my head. Sitting here were people with vast wealth. I don't resent them, it's just a world unfamiliar to me.

The difference at the breakfast table that was odd was the conversation never was about fishing. Lots of finance, a smattering of conservative politics, and from the wives some serious discussion of fashion trends. Turns out a guy named Jimmy Choo was very important in shoes. Turns out the pair worn across from me was worth more than the fly rods I brought. I smiled. I wondered if there would ever be a Jimmy Choo fishing shoe? I was ready to start fishing.

I met Bob at the breezeway of my chalet. That sounds so pretentious, it could only be worse if he came to pick me up in a limo. The river we would fish was about fifty yard from my door. I talked to Bob about fishing the river, the body of water to which the lodge is geared. Turns out that the river sans grasshoppers was extremely tough. That streamers offered some action. Any way you cut it, though, any way you try to describe it, the fishing was hard. There was another option. The river, as the water levels decline, creates some large and wonderful oxbow lagoons. Very large brown trout that are easy to see live here.

They used the term "fishing the lagoons." I love that term. For some reason it made me think of the silly 1960s sitcom *Gilligan's Island*. In the lagoons, you could fish terrestrials. That was the idea of it all. It was so pretty around the lagoons. Everything was so alien. You realize how conditioned we are to our flora and fauna. For me it was a wonderment. My favorite of all was the night sky. All my life I have looked up at the stars. The sky of the southern hemisphere is so different. It affects you. Then to make the whole thing even more boggling a comet was burning across the night sky my whole trip. It had many names—c/2006 P1, Comet McNaught, or the Great Comet of 2007. It is (as it is still careening through the universe) called a non-periodic comet. That it just has a trajectory unaffiliated with a cyclical gravitational force that would cause it to come back.

Comets are cool. They have been portents through all of man's known history and were probably even more powerful before. In my life, the promise of bright fiery celestial objects illuminating imaginations and skies always disappointed. My first recollection about comets was the hype and media frenzy that surrounded the Comet Kohoutek. In 1974 you could buy T-shirts and coffee mugs with the name Kohoutek on them, or even join the doomsday cult, Children of God. The comet foretold the beginning of the end. I even built a comet observation device out of a shoebox. Comet Kohoutek was a spectacular dud. Next was the coming of that old reliable stalwart in 1986, Halley's Comet. It visits every seventy-six years, right? All well documented and worth the hype. Except in 1986. Halley's was a shadow of its former self. Literally. It took the Great Comet of 2007 to show me what the reverential awe was about. With that comet blazing across the Southern Cross, in a place where no artificial light bled into the theatre of the sky, I couldn't help feeling some personal portent. All the events that led me to see it must have been for something. Kismet.

The trout in the lagoon were large. Some of the brown trout were well into the double digits. There is something about sight-casting big terrestrial flies to big trout. The issue was that the absence of the grasshoppers on the rivers put way more pressure on the lagoons. According to Bob, these fish were far easier to catch earlier in the year. All things being equal, he said, most of the guests were purist to the point where they *needed* to be mending lines in a current. Even in the present challenging conditions, most of the guests stuck to the river. Some had arranged float trips on rivers an hour or two away to get to different conditions and different fish. Even so, the lagoons were still receiving more pressure than usual. Even with the fishing pressure, I liked the lagoons. I even liked that the fish were educated and cagey. Having success on those terms reaffirms my acumen as a fly angler.

In the first couple of days, we exhausted all the different lagoons. Bob asked if I was ready for the river. I said I would stick to the lagoons. Some of the guests were glad that I wasn't taking a beat on the river. The fishing was tough and one more rod would not have helped. The other guests would make polite conversation at the evening "shows." They were strictly feeling me out. It's funny how wealthy people start to think that those in lower income brackets also possess lower IQs. I beat one guy nearly a half dozen times straight on the chess board. He just couldn't believe my luck. As Yogi Berra said, "Better to be lucky than good."

The shows in the lodge would take place after dinner. It was an odd, mostly torturous affair. One night they would sell very beautiful but pricey jewelry. From what I could gather it was silver, crafted locally. Another night it was alpaca goods. After the modified Tupperware party one of the ranch employees, Alexandrio, would break out his guitar and sing pop standards with his guitar case open. I would always be the first to throw some money in his case. He would beg a request, I would offer a Beatles tune. He loved the Beatles and was good at playing their songs. After the nightly fashion show and sale, and then a couple of Pisco Sours, a few Beatles songs—I was done. Escaping was never too easy, I would do a couple of familiar songs. Then I would request "In a Gadda da Vida" and our troubadour would smile and shrug his shoulders and I would say, "Well, I will come back when you learn it." I would pardon myself to bed and leave. It quickly became a running joke.

The thing about Patagonia, whether it is in Chile or Argentina, you will deal with the wind. It is your partner for all the fishing. A day without wind would be a memorable day— that I did not encounter. You learn to adapt to the wind and in some cases you even begin to use it. One day halfway through the trip, the wind swirled and threatened to change direction as it often does. On the swirling current my nose detected the whiff of something pungent with skunk overtones. Smell is a powerful catalyst to memory. The memory cells in my brain were working feverishly to get the smell in context. Just then, Bob stepped out of the brush near the bank I was fishing. "That smells like some good shit," I commented. There was a pause. Silence fell between the guide and his client. I am sure he was trying to figure out his next move. For him it could play out a number of different ways. Some not so good. For me, I was connecting the dots. He had been escaping regularly over the last few days. You have to wonder what kind of client you are that the guide has to get stoned while he is guiding you. During all this contemplating, the silence was growing heavier. "Hey man, don't sweat it. I am not going to say a word," I told him. Instantly my words seemed to crumble the worry that had furrowed his brow. Then he asked if I smoke.

That is one of those questions. I had not in almost twenty years. I had not even though about it in some time. I had remembered enjoying a nice buzz while fishing. Then I became a parent. I also lost some good friends to drugs. It took me a long time to realize that I did not lose my friends to drugs, but rather I lost them to themselves. In some recent contemplating I often thought as a very old man, when everything else stopped working, I could see myself getting high and fishing. This proposition was in my estimation about twenty-five years away. Then there is always that little voice in your head that says, "Why the fuck not?" This is the same voice that my cerebral brain had banished into some dark corner of my reptile brain. (Sometimes it escapes.) So I asked, "What do you have?"

Bob had some delicious black hash. I took several puffs and soon found myself very, very fucked up. It turns out that this was not your father's Oldsmobile. The potency of marijuana and related products (hashish is a product from compressed resin glands of the cannabis plant) had increased significantly since my casual Grateful Dead days. We ended up laughing a good amount. Some at my newly destroyed casting and the rest at silly shit high folks laugh at. It did allow me to end up bonding with Bob. In that time we started to talk about our personal lives and how fly fishing was important to each of us. It was his livelihood and it was how I could escape enough to bear my livelihood. I think he liked that the first time I got high in over twenty years was with him. On my part it established trust with my guide. Good things were bound to happen. As we drove back to the lodge for the evening, it seemed like he came to a decision about me: "Tomorrow I want to take you to a cool place. Tell the kitchen to pack us some lunches."

Part III

North Lake

It was the morning of our visit to the cool place. I thought it would be a good time to break out my tie-dye shirt. As I showed up for breakfast, you could hear the distinct pucker of nervous assholes clenching and unclenching. It probably had been a long time since these captains of industry broke bread with tie-dye-clad brethren. It probably made them uncomfortable. Maybe the same way they felt when Obama got elected. Shamefully, I secretly enjoyed it. Though I was not the dyed-in-the wool liberal they were imagining I was, I was not about to let them off the hook. It made the breakfast taste even better. At one point, Pinochet even moved his chair away a tad. All this over a colorful shirt.

After silence and a couple of throat clearings, the conversation began again. For the first time all week it was about fishing. It took collective guilt to bring up what fly to use in the absence of grasshoppers. Then the guides came in to collect their clients. As I looked at Bob, my delight was beyond measure. It seems my guide received the memo on tie-dye day. We looked at each other and smiled like colorful Cheshire cats. Kismet. He told me to get in the truck, we had a ride to take. As I got to the truck, I noticed it had a trailer with a Patagonian drift boat on it. I smiled some more. Bob wanted to show me this place so I felt it was going to be good.

There is an old saying: "She was uglier than nine miles of bad road." This was five times worse and uglier than that. The road was windy, dirty, craggy, rocky—and kept getting narrower and more harrowing up into the Andes Mountains. Eventually, we came upon a farm with a farmer at the gate. As he let us through, he also let out some real live gauchos. I was so amazed to see them. At the same time, I saw an ox pulling a cart and farm help using old wood pitch forks to heap straw into it. In a moment, I had slipped back in time more than a hundred years. I was told there were many who clung to the old ways. In a real way, it was close to a serf situation with our friend Pinochet as the lord. He even had a generator at the river, which created enough electricity so everyone in the nearby village was able to power one electric light bulb. The cost that led to relieve darkness at night was about five dollars a month. A hardship for most of the families.

Just past the gate, and down a ways, was the long and narrow lake. I would call it six miles long and maybe a little under a mile wide. Bob walked up next to me and held out his arms and introduced me: "Jerry, let me show you North Lake." She was beautiful. Her waters were blue with bands of milky jasper blue. Around the edges, it was clear with some sort of aquatic vegetation growing. It was windswept at this high altitude. The wind had not taken the day off.

Bob and the farmer wrestled the boat to the water. I kept smelling strawberry. Finally, I was less distracted and found the source of the smell. Little wild strawberries grew all over the place. While they dealt with the boat, I picked the sweetest little berries I had ever encountered.

Bob waved to me to come to the boat. I climbed in. I asked what I should tie on and he said, "It really doesn't matter—make it a terrestrial, a tough one."

I tied on a Nuclear Hopper. Mostly made of rubber in DayGlo yellow and orange, it was hideous and rugged. I used them for smallmouth bass. The wind, as it turned out, was whipping and blowing straight down the lake. It meant that Bob just had to keep me parallel with the shore and the wind would take us down the lake. I cannot tell you how many brown trout I caught that morning. It was more than one hundred and less than five hundred. By the time we stopped for lunch my mind was completely blown.

"Holy shit Bob, what was that?" I said.

"I told you it would be good." He smiled. "Can you believe I cannot get anyone to fish this? When I tell them it is a lake they turn me down."

"You mean I can fish this for my last two days?"

Bob laughed as he was lighting up some hashish. "Sure, hey you want some of this?"

"No way. I was so messed up. There wasn't a Twinkie for a thousand miles and I would have sold my soul for one. Having the munchies with caviar and paté on the table was not such a good scene."

Bob laughed and we ate our lunch. The afternoon was as good as the morning. I was just having trouble wrapping my brain around it. It was so much to take in. Okay, so I didn't catch anything bigger than three pounds. They had to be there, right? As any fisherman would do, I started formulating a strategy for the next day.

At the dinner table, someone asked how the lake was. I told them it was great and that I had plans to go there the next two days. I could feel wonky vibes coming from Pinochet. As I glanced at the man, he alternated in color from red to white to red. After dinner he sent his wife to give me the news. She told me that they had another lodge they operated. That the fishing had been very bad there and they were moving all the guests from this lodge to that one. I would not be able to fish North Lake again. In fact, I would be limited to fish the three pools adjacent to my chalet.

I said, "You mean for my last two days?"

She said yes, she was sorry. I said, "Bob said we could fish North Lake my last two days." I knew it was wrong when I said it.

I regretted bringing the guide into it almost immediately. She was getting frustrated. You could tell she got inserted in the middle of it and wished she was somewhere else.

"Look, I am very sorry about all this. It is just the way it is."

"So how much of my money are you refunding?" I asked.

She looked at me in disbelief. "What?"

I could sympathize with the other sports. If they were having such a bad run that they were willing to travel hours and sleep doubled up, the situation must have been really bad. In my mind, it seemed that all the patrons should have been warned. The grasshoppers not showing was clearly an act of God but the rest was an act of man. If it was my operation, I would have warned people and given them the opportunity to rebook the following season. In the meantime the "wife" walked away and was discussing things with her husband. He proceeded to summon Bob from the guide bunkhouse, pulling him into the middle of the show. The one where Alexandro had his guitar case open. Then he proceeded to rip Bob a new asshole in front of all the guests. Chiding him for setting up fishing assignments with guests and how would he like to get fired and sent back to "MOTANA" without pay? Poor Bob only looked at the floor. I was horrified for him. At the same time I looked at Pinochet. I could see his uncle in him. I could feel the rage seethe from him.

In that moment in the argument of nurture versus nature, nurture was losing. It seems DNA is hardwired and this guy had a dictator's heart. In some perverse way he thought tearing down this man in front of others was the thing to do. He clearly misunderstood Americans, as I looked around and the other guests were equally horrified. Almost at once the room started clearing. I stood up and inserted myself between Pinochet and Bob.

"I will fish with Bob those three pools for the next two days. Why would you do this? Asshole." With that I left.

The following morning, I ate my fruit and cheese. I skipped breakfast. Eventually Bob came to the door. I immediately apologized.

"Aww, that's okay," he said. "He does that often enough."

"That's awful. No one should have to eat that shit."

"Very few guide for him more than one season. He promised he would be better. I won't be back."

"Geez . . . I really didn't mean to get you in this. It just caught me off guard. You could fish those pools in two hours. That is really stretching it."

"Some of the other guests are leaving."

"It crossed my mind." Then I asked him how far away it would be for cell reception. He told me an hour's drive. I said let's go.

During that drive, I really got to know Bob. He was a good young man. All he wanted to be since he was a young boy was a fishing guide. Now he was living the dream. In many ways, I admired him. He was free. He was able to learn about and live in some of the best places to fish in the world. As my cell phone found a tower I placed a call to my friend Pat at The Fly Shop. The silence from his end spoke volumes. He told me he would make it right, even if it was when I got back home. I knew he would but I wanted him to help protect Bob a little. It turns out that many of the guides were sent there from The Fly Shop to help them work through the offseason. Having the American guides was a boon to Pinochet and through that affiliation he would try to help Bob as well.

That evening after dinner, Bob asked if he could talk to me outside.

"What's up?" I said.

Through his smile, he told me: "Well, we are going back to North Lake tomorrow."

"Really?" I said as I was looking up at the great comet. It was bright and beautiful. It was a portent to the last day.

The ride to North Lake was fraught with the same terror. I think Bob put a little extra twist to it. I had the feeling it was going to be quite a day. The wind was really roaring. I had the Payne rod strung up. I switched to a lighter Dave Whitlock hopper. A fish hit the very first cast. The wind carried us down the lake. It was different as it would blow us slightly offshore so that Bob would have to adjust and move us in. The one thing we did notice, the farther offshore we went, the bigger the trout got. We pulled over for lunch. If possible we caught even more fish than the time before.

"Hey Bob, why don't we try a few drifts a bit farther out? The fish seem a little bigger I think."

"Yeah, I was noticing that too. Did you pick any of them strawberries? I am going to need them here in a bit." He said as he filled his pipe. "Do you want some?"

I said, "Without any Twinkies, it would just be impossible."

Bob had this giant grin lighting up his whole face. He then reached into his duffle bag and proceeded to produce a whole box of Hostess Twinkies.

"You son of a bitch." I laughed. "I guess we do it your way."

I took a couple of tiny hits. I was trying to modify the intensity of it all. That afternoon was the best brown-trout fishing I ever had. The drift farther out with Whitlock's hopper was the pattern I was looking for. The average fish went from three to five pounds. Then, later in the afternoon, an enormous head poked up to take my fly. I pulled back to set the hook. It was a heavy fish. Bob was doing all he could to keep the boat in the wind. You could hear the Payne moan under the pressure. The fish was played with patience and delicacy and the guide practiced boat control under difficult windy conditions. Eventually, the nine-pound-plus brown was netted. That was it. After it was released, I broke down my rod and put away my reel.

"Let's just drift down the lake for a bit," I said.

"Don't you want to fish anymore?" Bob replied in his guide's voice.

"I just finished the best day of trout fishing in my life the way I wanted it to end."

There is truth in proper endings. As I sat there with the wind blowing in my face, I wondered how long it would be before a similar day happened. I thought this was one of my halcyon days. How rare it is to feel it in the moment. Mostly we wander through our memories and award them years later.

That evening, the traditional formal dinner would be replaced by a local tradition. They call it an *Asada*. They roast a whole lamb, side of beef, chicken, corn, and potatoes. Some gauchos from the village played cultural music. The alcohol flowed. It seemed that all was forgotten and the tension was gone. I looked up at the great comet and felt the wonder of my place in this universe.

Chapter 12:
Touch of Grey

"The shoe is on the hand it fits,
There's really nothing much to it,
Whistle through your teeth and spit,
'Cause it's all right.

Oh well, a touch of grey
kind of suits you anyway.
That was all I had to say,
It's all right."
— *"Touch of Grey" by Grateful Dead*

If you do something long enough, and it is worthy, you begin to yearn for the roots. You want to find the foundation. Eventually, it kicks off a journey to search for moral or spiritual significance. A pilgrimage of sorts. Pilgrimages usually mean a journey to a shrine or a place of personal importance. The journey can also be metaphorical. The best are both. If you fly fish, your journey at one point must be to the Catskill Mountains town of Roscoe, New York. Some will argue for the blue-ribbon staple streams of the

American West. In the end, you have to look toward New York's Beaverkill, Willowemoc, and Delaware River and its branches.

As a young man, I chose to go to college in Oneonta, New York—about ninety minutes from the legendary Junction Pool in Roscoe. I loved to fly fish. I knew that the Catskills were home to some good water. Foolish stubbornness in youth would force me to say it was almost as good as the water at home, near Rochester, New York. I never could have realized when I went there how much it was part of what I loved. The fly-fishing culture was all over that place. At first, jaded by Madison Avenue campaigns, I figured that must be a small-town sales pitch. Yet I ended up near there by some metaphysical accident. I fished around Roscoe often in the brazen, bold manner of youth. I met and talked to fishing legends. I even had sense enough to pester Lee Wulff into signing a book of flies for me. After all this, it took years to trace back my steps. To finally get it all right and in perspective. Looking back now, I was like a kid in Jerusalem playing handball up against the Wailing Wall.

When you come to Roscoe, New York, you feel the culture instantly. It must have been the feeling guys like Theodore Gordon, Rube Cross, and AE Hendrickson had when they tightened lines there. If you go now, make sure you set aside time to visit The Catskill Fly Fishing Center and Museum. It really helps frame things. For years I favored the Beaverkill. (By the way, *kill* is the Dutch word for river or water channel; so the name essentially means *beaver river*.) More recently, I have been favoring the Willowemoc. Willowemoc Creek has been drawing fishermen since the railroad allowed access in the mid 1870s. It is about twenty-seven miles long and really has three personalities. The top section is cold and clear and here the stream is small. It is full of wild brook trout and the occasional brown trout. The middle section is a bit wider and slower and the catch tends to be even between the brookies and the browns. The lower stretch is bigger and slower; it has large classic pools that let dry flies dance on the water like a dream. There is a 2.4-mile no-kill zone in this southern stretch that holds almost all my attention now when I go. This is a forgiving place. It is here I become the best flyfisher I can be. Late spring is a vibrant time on the Willowemoc. The water is still ice cold but the air temperature is warm enough that you can shed some of the heavier clothing needed just a week or two earlier.

I like to get on the water in the first or second week of May to catch the Red Quill (a type of mayfly) hatch. I don't think it is a major hatch or even one with a big following. The reason why I like it is probably something science can't prove. I have noticed the trout really grab these bugs—the fish pounce hard and grab tight, which makes for better hook sets and more fish landed. In my mind, I think these must be exceptionally delicious Red Quills. I know there is no way to prove this. One time, many years ago, I did offer a friend who would eat almost anything some money to eat a Red Quill. Regrettably, he informed me that he was past that stage in life and I could keep my five bucks. Fish do hang onto some bugs better than others. It has to be because they are delicious. Right?

The other thing I like about fishing here: You can use large flies. There seem to be two distinctive hatches—one in a size 14 (the smaller size) and the other in a size 12. I like the size 12 because I like catching big trout on big flies. It is nice to see nature in large and clear pictures. Some friends of mine seem to need to know exactly what bug is hatching. For me, the term "Red Quill" is enough. I do know that the hatch here is in the *Ephemerella* family. Maybe they are *subvaria* and maybe they are not. The entomology is not important to me. There is a guy who used to fish in some of the same circles as I did. Bug entomology and the proper Latin names became very important to him. In the end, he stopped bringing a rod and only had a dip net. When people ask me about him all I can say is he went "buggy."

Other fishermen I know feel the need to identify the precise Latin name of the hatch they are trying to match. That in some way it gives them power over the situation. I took Latin in high school and forgot most of it soon after. I memorized the simple phrase *culus aeni*. When pressed I say that is the hatch I believe is happening. When I see other anglers totally puzzled, I add that the bugs are a bronzy color. (It is vulgar slang. It means bronze asshole. I guess being force-fed a dead language in a Jesuit high school was bound to lead to the memorization of such uselessness. The irony, though, is that I have found a use.) Occasionally, I do get a rebuff. I usually just smile and apologize.

The Red Quills are a rusty brown color with a hint of red. The best imitations are tied with medium bronze dun hackle barbs. Even that is too technical for me. I am probably the worst fly tier that ever lived. I tried tying dry flies. I did master the San Juan Worm. Anyway, I learned about color and some materials, as I have to be specific with those who can tie, who I coax into tying me what I need. Most fly tiers use a catalog approach and you deal with that. It leaves me scouring fly shops and tiers for what I think is close to the imitation I want. I have a large collection of flies. I find it easy to bring a fly to a guy and say, "Here, I need two dozen of these." Over the years, I've found a few tiers who indulge me. In a way, it is like using a police sketch artist. I sit there as they whip off fly after fly, allowing me to give them gradual modifications. Most guys would choke the shit out of you for doing that. Think about it. So I've been lucky. I have also resorted to buying antique flies at auctions.

The Red Quill hatch usually happens on miserable days. If it's a slow, steady drizzle, I know the action will be good. It seems the grayer the day, the better the hatch will be.

This day was cooperative. It was still and gray. The cloud ceiling was low and moving slow. It felt like rain. My knees are arthritic and seem to ache when the humidity is very high. A slight chill had the tip of my nose cold; it was nippy. The no-kill fishing stretch had a few fishermen on it so it would be easy to find a spot to cast. I slipped into the Willowemoc and the familiar fishing rhythm was not difficult to find. The history of the place seeps into your psyche and you cast a little more carefully to impress the ghosts of the cane-rod club's past members. It's not long before you can see the early signs of the hatch beginning. The nice thing about the place is that even though it gets lots of attention, it never gets fished too hard. If you get things correct you will be rewarded with fish. It wasn't long before browns were hitting my flies.

I noticed the guy about fifty yards downstream. He seemed to be very old and frail. He was standing in a good spot that was easy to wade. I remember thinking that he must know the place a little. It's funny that in most of life, away from fishing, I don't pay any attention to what people are wearing. When I hear a report about the fashion faux pas that occurred on the red carpet at a Hollywood event, I wonder how people keep track. Then I think about being on a stream. I notice everything. I can usually tell quite a bit from what a guy brings to the stream. The gentleman below me was obviously old school. His old canvas waders told me a lot. They were probably from the 1960s but appeared to be in good shape. He was fishing a flamed bamboo rod of some kind. He was still too far away to get the particulars down.

After a while, I did notice something else. He was not catching fish. It is always a dilemma on a stream. Do you offer help or do you mind your own business? I am always willing to help but I am also very sensitive about not invading space. Often, I go fishing as a way to run from trouble. Sometimes it's nice to put a little time and distance between you and your demons. During those times, I don't want to talk to anyone. I looked at him again. He looked very old. He was probably doing this before I was born. I decided I would leave him be.

A couple hours passed and the fishing was respectable. I landed a brown trout that was all of twenty inches. That seems to be the benchmark size for these waters. I did notice that the elderly man had not hooked one fish all morning. The chill of the day was getting to me. I often keep a Thermos of strong, hot coffee with me streamside. Sometimes I even enjoy making cowboy coffee with a small fire. That would be impossible here so the Thermos was the way. I grabbed it and headed toward where the old man was fishing. I found a rock to sit on and poured a cup. The old man was in shouting distance and I yelled to ask if he'd like a cup. He looked up and considered the offer. A few moments later he was leaning against my rock with his hand ready to grasp a warm cup of Joe.

As he leaned his rod against the other side of the rock, I noticed an oversize Adams tied on his tippet. We exchange greetings and names. He is Calvin. Up close, he looks even older. He is holding the warm cup close, breathing the coffee vapors, enjoying the aroma and the heat. I am doing the same. It is quiet for a bit. Hot coffee chasing the chill out of grown men is a simple, quiet pleasure. There are times it is good to let it be just that. After the thaw he speaks.

"I notice you had a good morning. The Red Quill hatch seems to be coming off nicely."

"You get that? So why the big Adams?" I asked.

"It took me a half an hour to tie that on last night. My fingers won't let me tie streamside. I tied on the smallest Adams I could. I have always had fair luck with an Adams."

I took out my clippers and snipped the Adams off his line. I tied on one of my size 12 Red Quills. I could relate, in relative terms. I don't mess around with anything much smaller than a size 24 anymore. That is probably a lie. Maybe it is a size 22, these days. I looked at him as he watched me tie the fly to his line. I tested the knot and it failed. I realized the tippet was no good either. I had some questions forming but politeness kept me silent. I put on a new leader and tied on a fresh tippet and then the fly. He watched and smiled. I looked into his eyes and saw an impatience that was new. He dumped the rest of his coffee and headed back to the water. I think I even detected a spring in his step. "Thank you, sir!" he said.

I moved upstream and began to fish my spot. As I took the fly from the hook holder, I heard a *whoop* from Calvin. He had just landed a nice trout. I spent much of the afternoon facing him and watching. It was clear he was old school. The really old school guys keep the elbow of their rod arm touching their ribs while casting. It is like they have a belt tied around their arm just above the elbow and around the chest. It is a tight-to-the-body style of casting with most of the action in the wrist. It is clean and conservative of motion. In many ways, it prevents bad habits from creeping in. On the downside, it looks rigid and lacks a certain flair. The final analysis is that he was accurate and caught fish. Catching fish always is a mood enhancer. Later in the afternoon he headed toward me.

He motioned that I come out of the water. I went to the bank and saw his fly was chewed up pretty good. He offered to trade me a cheap cigar if I would tie on a fresh fly. I told him I would skip the cigar but would be delighted to tie on a new fly. I handed him the beat up one and he proceeded to carefully take off his cap and place the fly in the band. It was an old felt roll-up Fedora. The Red Quill looked just right in the band. He told me if I wouldn't take the cigar he would have to buy me dinner. I said that would be just fine.

I guess there are several places to eat in this area. But unless otherwise specified, any meeting for food is automatically implied to be at the Roscoe Diner. It is a 1950s vintage diner, even though it was built in 1964. It's famous in its own right but is legendary in sporting circles. If you think you're going to have breakfast there opening day, you'd better arrive very early. It sits right on Route 17 and is as famous among flyfishermen as any eating establishment. The French toast is worth writing home about.

I grabbed a table and waited for Calvin, who eventually worked his way in. Out of his fishing clothes he looked frail and weak. He grabbed the edge of the table and eased into the booth. His hair was yellow, the color past white. I looked at him and smiled. I told him that he seemed to do well in the afternoon and that tomorrow would be a better day.

"No, it won't." He spoke in a thin voice. "Today is it. It is the last day of fly fishing in my life." I must have looked puzzled. "Ah," he said, "it's okay. This life doesn't owe me anything. The truth is I am dying. I have prostrate cancer and it is terminal."

What do you say? In my case, I had recently survived non-Hodgkin's lymphoma and began to tell him about my trials. That if I could get past The Beast he could too. He let me know that he was familiar with The Beast. (The Beast is what cancer is called in cancer-patient circles. It has a ring that seems to fit.)

"I beat this cancer twice. Maybe just beat it back is a better way of saying it. My doctors said I am too old and frail for treatment. I barely got today in. I was glad you were there to help me. Catching those trout is how I wanted to remember my last day."

There was an awkward silence. What could I say? The waitress came to the table to take our orders. As we looked up at her something hung in the air. It must have been thick as she glanced back and said it looked like we weren't ready yet. She was right. Calvin broke the stalemate.

"You know I am ninety-two, and if I can hang on for another month I will make ninety-three. I was a child in the Depression, fought in the World War, survived both my sons, my wife, two rounds of cancer, and I have run my race."

We ordered dinner and the conversation went on. I found out he was on a boat at the Normandy invasion. He married his high-school sweetheart. They had two sons. The first was what he called a "hippy." Apparently he struggled with drug addiction and was an early HIV victim. His other son died more recently of heart disease. He felt that his wife passed of a broken heart after the second boy died. He could remember the first canned beer, ballpoint pen, freeze-dried coffee, Aerosol cans, the Slinky, the Atomic Bomb, Tupperware, Superglue, Mr. Potato Head, the Pill, Fortran, the artificial heart, and the Frisbee. We talked about all these things. We talked about life. He was an intelligent man. Owned his own insurance business. He told me that love was the most important thing. Hate was the great destroyer. Then things came full circle to fishing.

Calvin was a real old-time flyfisherman. He told me about how he fished here just after coming home from the War. That he took six months off just to fish. How that was considered radical back then. You were expected to get your life going. He didn't want to elaborate but he needed healing. That the landing at Normandy was carnage without words. The little bits he did share caused his tired old eyes to well up.

So I said: "You became a short-term trout bum."

He looked at me for a second. "No. I was never no bum! I just needed some time. I worked my whole life. No, I was never no bum."

I was trying to bring some levity to the table. It just wasn't going to happen then. We chatted some more and as dinner wound down it seemed like there were still words that needed saying. Prolonging and crafting the epilogue seemed important. We agreed that I would pick up Calvin in front of his motel room. We would go to a local watering hole and share a few beers in a style that men have been doing since beer was first hoisted.

I pulled up at the motel and Calvin was waiting. He waved and came to the car. Getting in took a moment. I was wondering if I could make it to ninety-three? You push thoughts of mortality aside. It becomes more difficult when you are in the company of someone who has no choice but to look it straight on. I wondered how long he had. Being a cancer patient myself, I can tell you that is the one question you never ask. It is too personal and painful. The other question people would ask is, "Is it terminal?" Fucking awful question. I know people were just at a loss. Most never meant any harm.

Calvin was in his seat and we started to the bar. It was a twenty-minute drive. He was telling me about places he had fished. I asked how fishing had changed over the years. He felt overall it was better now. The biggest loss was unspoiled habitat and under-pressured fish. That you could still have those things but you had to go much farther now. That the current notion of conservation really saved things. His recollection of the 1960s was that it hurt the outdoors. That by the '70s, the current culture of conservation rose out of necessity. In the background I had a homemade CD playing. He heard and recognized "Smoke gets in your eyes . . ."

"I never heard this singer," Calvin said, "but I like it." I explained it was Leon Russell and that I burned my own CDs because my music tastes were all over the board. He started to listen a little closer. Before long we were at the local watering hole.

As we got past the neon Budweiser signs and your eyes adjusted to the dim bar light, you could see the patrons. It was a dual-purpose bar. It served both the locals and transient fishermen. It was easy to spot who was whom. We knew instantly what side we should sit on. Conversation took up where it left off at dinner. We talked about many things. How once it was easy to tell the good guys from the bad. When a movie was shown the good guys wore white; the bad guys wore black. The world was easy. Superman was a role model and Solomon Grundy was not. That in this world, those lines have become so blurry. I think as we all age we get lost in the cultural difference.

Listening to Calvin, I began to wonder if he wasn't on to something? Have we gone too far in complicating our lives?

"Happiness is much harder to find in a culture of entitlement," he said. Calvin told me that one of the benefits of knowing the approximate hour of your demise is you can put your life in perspective. He had for the most part reconciled it all. That today's trout were some of the last things he wanted to do one more time and did. It was getting late and we were winding down.

"You know," he said, "I would like to hear that song again when we go back."

"Smoke gets in your eyes?" I said.

"No, not that one. The one where the refrain is 'I will survive.' He keeps singing about a touch of gray in his hair."

"That song is called 'Touch of Grey,'" I said. "I would be glad to play it."

On the ride back I played it for him and could see he was taking it all in. We spoke almost not at all. So much had been said that it seemed more would be too much. We listened to the music on the way back.

As we got nearer to the motel he spoke again: "I should have paid more attention to music. There are songs on that CD I really don't care for but there are some I never heard before and are, well, just really something."

I ejected the CD and handed it to him. He looked at me. "No, no I couldn't take it." I told him no worries, I would just burn another one. I told him I really wanted him to have it.

"That song. 'Touch of Grey.' If you don't mind I want to tell you something. They tell you when you are in your twenties it doesn't get any better. That's a god-damned lie. The twenties were awful, but things gradually got better. You get more confident with age and there is a time it all balances. Where you are the sharpest tool you will ever be. I look at you and see the touch of grey at your temples. Let me tell you: You are at the top. Don't mistake it and don't waste it. When he says a touch of grey kind of suits you anyway . . . he is talking about being cock of the walk. Strut boy! Make sure you strut." He fell silent for a minute. "I have something I want to show you." He got out of the car and I followed him.

He slowly trudged toward his shiny Buick. He motioned me to come to the back of it. Soon he had the trunk open. His old wrinkled hands searched the large trunk until they found what he sought. I looked at him and he was silhouetted by the streetlight behind him. I could make out a rod case and the faint bronze cap at the end. He held it out to me. I grabbed it. I might have gone through the motions of saying it was too much. I didn't: I knew what was happening. I was being bequeathed a sentimental gift. Something that one fisherman could only give to another. It was more than a rod. It was heavy in the way that could not be scripted. I could feel my tongue tighten and my eyes water. I could not speak but only shake my head. I took the rod and pounded my chest over my heart. My eyes were tearing and so were his.

I walked to my car, rod in hand. I could only wave and he waved back. I drove to my room knowing that was it. We had a friendship of one day. One good day. I sat in the chair and held the rod case. I ran my finger across it. It was beautiful. It was brass covered in leather. His initials were embossed near the top. CK. It made me think of Calvin Klein. I would never know what the K stood for.

I have spent many moments looking at that case. I have not opened it. At first I didn't want to, believing Calvin may still be with us. It just didn't feel right. It has been some time and I still look at the case when I am going through my fishing stuff. As I look in the mirror and notice the touch of gray becoming more pronounced, Calvin's words echo in my head. In some ways they frighten me. I know soon I will have to reconcile it all and fish with Calvin's rod. I owe him that.

We go on these pilgrimages in our lives looking for different kinds of truths. Some we are ready to face and they reaffirm things. Sometimes it becomes more than we bargained for. A very old man, knocking on heaven's door, gave me more than a rod. He gave me perspective. Sometimes I think way down I am still that boy. The one who keeps metaphysically playing handball on the Wailing Wall. By some instinctive compass-finding direction from ghosts of the past. I guess that is why I keep standing in water, fishing. As it washes over me in a baptism of sorts, I often find what I need.

Chapter 13:
Finding a Sanctuary

"Finding a sanctuary, a place apart from time, is not so different from finding a faith."

—*Pico Iyer*

When you listen to the Beatles song "Let It Be" you know it is about finding peace in a sea of trouble. Trouble is an overused word. The modern media seem to use it to get our attention to elevate their ratings. My grandfather used to say, "If you think you have trouble, write it down, and mail it to yourself. If it is still sitting on your chest when you open that letter, then it's trouble." He was right.

I have no problem saying I have opened a few trouble letters to myself. A small percentage of those qualified. I opened the first one, ever, when I was eleven. I was born with a hole in my heart and surgery was approaching. I had known it was coming for years, but it only became relevant when a date was assigned. I opened the letter, read it, and cried. In searching for ways to deal with trouble, I unwittingly stumbled on the concept of sanctuary. Turns out there are two kinds.

The first kind is a diversion from sorrow. I mastered this one early in life. I found fly fishing. Having been indoctrinated into fishing from my earliest memories, it was easy to part with the three dollars to purchase a Fenwick fly-fishing "kit" at a neighborhood garage sale. It was in its original packaging and had never been opened. It was clearly intended to be an entry-level introduction to fly fishing. It consisted of a 4-weight-ish fiberglass rod, a simple reel, and some awful flies.

The early fiberglass rods provided fast casting actions. This particular rod came nowhere close to that. It was painfully slow. Being self-taught on a very, very slow fly rod did to my casting what being left handed in a Catholic school did to my penmanship. In the end it worked out. I eventually and unwittingly prepared myself for fishing bamboo by casting that fiberglass rod. As for the penmanship, schools don't even teach cursive writing anymore. I still write notes and letters and send them with an actual stamp via the U.S. postal system. Being a dinosaur can be fun.

This type of diversion was fine—but I found that the sorrow comes flooding back when you stop the diversion.

The second kind of sanctuary helps you *heal* from sorrow. This is real sanctuary, the one that helps heal your soul and is hard to come by in life. In the end it didn't last as long as I needed it to.

It all started in my early twenties. I was only a couple years out of college and the little family I had started was shattered to pieces. Looking back, American television was truly a disservice for me. My parents were separated by the time I was two. I would watch all the family shows hoping for a *Brady Bunch* outcome. It was years before I learned Mr. Brady was gay and Mrs. Brady was sleeping with Greg. At the time, I didn't know this and felt the crush of family failure in my own life. I had this overwhelming feeling to run away.

The first thought was to go to a fishing lodge. The fly-in kind, in Northern Ontario, could be far enough away to escape the reality of life. I managed to get my hands on a Northern Ontario tourism booklet that listed all the lodges in Ontario. I called around and found one that would take me as soon as I could get there. I had to drive north to the fly-in base. It was about fourteen hours. My car had a new cassette deck. I drove straight through. I arrived the following morning and walked through the door. I went to the counter and told the man who I was. He smiled and talked about a bat out of hell, took my money, and told me to go down to the dock. As it was, he had the plane loaded with groceries for the lodge. If I didn't mind sitting next to a sack of onions, he said, I could be fishing in a few hours.

Being knocked off center compromises your judgment about almost everything. As I stood there on the dock at the lodge, I realized I was in the Arctic watershed and I hadn't told anyone where I was, with two rods and three day's worth of clothes, for a week's fishing.

I ambled onto the plane and we took off heading to Whitewater Lake. On future trips, I would notice details such as the kind of plane or how long the flight was. On this flight, I just noticed my shoes—how I had paid so much for this pair of Walter Dyer moccasins and they missed a stitch. It seemed important.

Some places are imbued with a force that reaches out to us from some unknown point in the universe. Ogoki Lodge was a big log structure with guest cabins around it. The story was the Canadian government had built it for the natives in the area and they tired of it and sold it to my host Bill and his wife. Bill was a good guy and the staff was accommodating. The lodge was built in the shape of a giant teepee and one of the breakfast dishes was teepee eggs. Cut a round hole in a piece of toast and place it over an egg sunny side up. Then make a teepee with two more pieces of toast. I also remember the beds, which took you in like comforting arms. We remember shards of things and deep sleep was one of the Whitewater shards.

I wasn't the only one who thought the place was special. The odd scientist, Wendell Beckwith, thought it to be the center of the universe.

Wendell Beckwith was an inventor and scientist who worked for the Parker Pen Company. Feeling dissatisfied with the rat race and wanting to work on something more satisfying than ink flow, he decided to give up his contract with Parker, set up a trust fund for his wife and five children, and disappear. Taking inspiration from Einstein, he believed he needed to be free from other thinkers so as to pursue and craft astronomical, mathematical, and gravitation theorems. In 1961, he calculated that the center of all was right on Best Island in the middle of Whitewater Lake. He built an architectural wonder there. It was a three-building compound all hand hewn by Beckwith. Every joint was dovetailed into the next. The kitchen featured a wooden cooler that would lower into the ground with a pulley system. One building had large wooden hexagonal floors and was heated by a 35-ton fireplace. It might have been the most inaccessible architectural wonder on the continent. One year Beckwith built a replica of Stonehenge on the ice, using trees to represent the stones. He grew food on his island and neighboring islands and was self-sufficient. He died in 1980 and left everything to the province of Ontario. There are people still working on his math. So far it is impossible to tell if he was crazy or a genius. History has shown that to be a very fine line.

Either way, the place had some magic—had to, for Beckwith to invest all that time. I could feel it too. As for the fishing? The place was rich in walleyes. That first time I took two fishing rods with me—a spinning rod and a fly rod. I used the spinning rod for the walleyes. I know some guys are so hard-core, the thought of holding a spinning rod is anathema. They would go so far as to put a minnow on a sink-tip line to dredge for walleyes. Someone invented the noodle rod to fill the gap between fishing methods. Still, there are those who just can't do the spinning thing.

Oddly enough, one of the guys I'm talking about is a dyed-in-the-wool AMC man as well. The good thing is I can always tell when he's fishing by the blue AMC Pacer parked at the turnout. The bad thing is the nervous breakdown he will suffer when he can no longer get his car repaired. Again, crazy or genius, I can't tell.

I brought the fly rod in case I found pike. I knew there would be pike and pike are funny, mean, glorious fish. I lump pike into two categories—the good and the bad. The bad pike have lots of names, such as hammer handles, snot rockets, slime sticks, johnnies, and head bangers. I like the term head banger the best. It really captures them in their entirety. A head banger is a pike that attains a length between eighteen and twenty-six inches and is tubular. Basically, it looks like three coke cans taped together. I have been in places where you can catch them cast after cast. They are voracious eating machines. A mindless tubular stomach with razor-sharp teeth and no fear. The real problem is that you can get into a place where either all the big ones have been removed or the fishery is stunted.

I remember having contests with friends as a young man where we tried to find the most ridiculous lure on which to catch them. These are actual qualifiers: a beer can, sweat sock, condom, cheese Danish, Weeble (a children's toy—a Weeble wobbles but it won't fall down), a ping-pong ball, and a Barbie doll's head. I am sure there are more but you get the point. At first these fish are fun, like an eager girlfriend, but eventually you wonder when she will stop calling.

The good-size pike have cool names like water wolf, swamp shark, gators, and depth dragons. These are northern pike over thirty inches. Something happens to them. They get meaner and moodier. They can be aggressive but seldom stupid. They can inflict a wound that requires hospitalization. Flyfishermen seldom receive scars from the sport so when we do it is the epitome of cool. I mean, if you overheard an Orvis guy talking to an L.L. Bean guy about the scar he has on the last joint of his index finger from abrasions caused by fly line—how cool would it be to walk over and say you couldn't have a scar like that because a northern pike took off the top of your index finger just below the first joint? I think there is something exciting about fishing for a species where that scenario is possible. If you look in the water at the fish and think, "I am really going to have to be careful"—that is the definition of a good pike.

Eventually, in the course of travelling between walleye holes, I stumbled upon the spot. Canadian shield lakes are hell on outboard lower units. Props and skegs are usually banged up good. I even keep a couple of extra sheer pins in my fly box. You learn to go slow and pay attention. As such, I was intensely scanning the water ahead. It wasn't a rock that caught my eye, it was the vast cabbage weeds just under the surface. Cabbage weeds are to big northern what a den is to a lion.

I stopped, looked, and calculated that I was seeing about three acres of dense cabbage weeds. Many factors have to come together for a patch like that to occur so far north. I know what it means. I quickly make mental notes and then write it down. On a lake this large, this is a needle in a haystack.

I stop the boat and rig up the fly rod. On the end of the tippet I tie on a Hooty Mama, in a blue-and-red variation. I just know what is going to happen.

I make a long cast and use a zigzag retrieve. Then it *does* happen—the part of fishing for big pike that I love: the wake the predator causes as it closes in on its prey. Pushing a V-shaped column of water, the wolf gets to the fly. You see a flash of white as it opens its maw. The setup is not delicate and the fight begins. The fish fights for its life and I fight for sport. At first it seems unfair. Then you realize the pike has inflicted this kind of flight response many times in his toothy life. It comes to the net—all of eighteen pounds. Subsequent casts produce similar fish. As I am standing on the seat casting the big fly to big fish, I am alone. Even with other people at the lodge, no one else is within miles. Being alone and feeling good, I felt like Linus in the pumpkin patch. Charles M. Schulz was the author of the *Peanuts* comic strip. More people on the planet have read his comic strip than have read Shakespeare. I am not sure how that illuminates current culture but it does speak to Schulz's genius in connecting with the human condition.

So there I was in the cabbage patch, in the center of the universe, maybe. And it happened. The wake caused by the displacement of water is large. The flash of white unmistakable. The hook set is solid. Rock solid.

At first the fish came to the boat with ease. It was the same feeling you get bringing a kite back to Earth. Then I saw the fish. When your knees go weak for the first time, all the clichés become understandable. It was a behemoth. Well over fifty inches.

Once the fish saw the boat, the fight was on. In a serpentine manner it easily cruised away from the boat. I knew my 6-weight and I were fucked. I did my best to gingerly play the fish. Twenty minutes into the fight, the giant took flight. It jumped out of the water just to show its massive girth, and on the down stroke, with a massive thrust of its tail . . . shattered my rod. It was over. I was Ahab and he was Moby Dick.

That was more than twenty-five years ago and the memory still haunts me to this day. I sat down for a long while just to feel and process it all—what had brought me to the cabbage weed patch at the top of the world. Around the corners it felt all right. That it would be all right.

Over the years I would come to my "pumpkin patch" to find sanctuary. Hoping the Great Pumpkin pike would return.

In my life, I've hooked plenty of pike in the twenty- to twenty-five-pound range; but I never hooked a pike nearly that large again. It doesn't matter.

When my fishing buddy Dave was killed in a car crash, I went north. When my heart was broken for one reason or another, I went north. The isolation and the effects of the center of the universe always managed to soothe me. One trip after I had come out from the wilderness, I was happy and standing at a gas pump. I asked the attendant if there was anything going on. He said, "Yeah, you guys are at war."

"What?" I responded.

"Bush invaded Kuwait," he said. I was conflicted in the fact that it didn't feel bad. Later I would figure out I was still awash in the protection of my sanctuary. In time, as I was home and under the media umbrella, my patriotic heart felt it all.

For years that place was good sanctuary. It helped me heal and move on. As the saying goes, "All good things must end." So too did my place. Ogoki Lodge failed—these are hard businesses at which to succeed. The guy who owns Adam's Mark hotels purchased all the other lodges in the area. He had an Aussie girlfriend many years his junior and thought it would be nice to give her a part of the world. They ran it like a big corporation and fucked it up. Isn't that what big corporations do? Eventually the former host Jack died and I found a way to get back. I did manage to find that beautiful patch of cabbage weeds and it was as wonderful as ever. Somehow something had changed. Maybe the center of the universe moves. Perhaps it creeps along like the continents. It was like the time I worked with this woman. I was madly in love. It was easily the deepest crush I ever had. Then one day she came in with much shorter hair. All the love, lust, and infatuation were gone. Just like that. It was the same with my place of sanctuary. I spent a week there and it was gone. Just like that. I am forever grateful for the power it extended to heal me.

Good sanctuary has that. I wonder if Wendell Beckwith was alive, would he feel it too? It doesn't matter.

In thinking about it all I have come to the conclusion that there have to be other places. I just need to find one that works for me. I have been looking for some time now. I suppose if these places came easy, they would be less special. In the search has come a kind of sanctuary, too. More along the lines of the distracting kind: the continued search forms a quest; the quest itself is a fine thing. How we have such a quest within the Odyssey of life. It may not be the search for the Holy Grail. Nonetheless, it is romantic.

Chapter 14:
Catch the Blue Train

Yeah, I can see it now
The distant red neon shivered in the heat
I was feeling like a stranger in a strange land
You know where people play games with the night
God, it was too hot to sleep
I followed the sound of a jukebox coming from a levee
all of a sudden I could hear someone from right behind me
I turned around and she said
"Why do you always end up down at Nick's café?"
I said "I don't know, the wind just kind of pushed me this way."
She said "Hang the rich."
Catch the blue train
To places never seen before
look for me
Somewhere down the crazy river
(Somewhere down the crazy river)
Catch the blue train

—*Lyrics by Robbie Robertson*

In life, we have different strands that get intertwined. If we are lucky, how we work and how we play and how we love come together in a seamless masterpiece. My life is not like that. I suspect most lives are not. I have read about people who seem to have it all. I suspect upon closer inspection the illusion dissipates. In my life there are moments in which those element do come together, in brief conjunctions of memorable interludes. Looking back, they are milestones that mark time in a life. Some are especially good.

For a large chunk of my life, I was road manager for a stand-up comedian. I spent twenty-eight years working for and with George Carlin. It wasn't my only job but it was a good one. Road Manager sounds like a hell of a title. In fact, it was. It was also the low man on the road. Most of the grunt work fell to me. I had to get to each gig early and ensure setup. Check stage, sound, and lights. I was responsible for box-office duties. I was the first guy there and the last guy to leave. At the height of things, we were on the road a good 250 days a year. I had a driver (who was also the swag guy) and we would travel everywhere in a big SUV. The great part was I always managed to fit a rod or gun or bow case in there somewhere. It was a wonderful ride that ended abruptly with the passing of my friend in June 2008.

Next, I became president of the Cat Fanciers Association. It is an elected position for a two-year term. I am in my second term as I write this. As president of CFA I get to travel all over the globe. Again I find that I manage to have a rod case as often as not. Human beings are funny in that they are very resourceful. It was in organizing my thoughts for this story that I realized that I figured out how to hunt and fish the whole planet without actually having it in my mission statement. "Clever bastard," I thought.

George and crew were going to play Mobile, Alabama, on a Saturday night and we had a rare Sunday off. We would not have to be back on the road until the following Thursday. I was always mindful when I was close enough to New Orleans. I have always had a love affair with the Big Easy. It is everything—I am a jazz fanatic; the food; the French Quarter; the whole thing is so good. (Before Katrina it was rapture. I have not been back since—for no reason other than I am afraid. I am planning to see it soon.) The thought of three days was so good. In college, several of my fraternity brothers and I rented a small two-bedroom apartment in the French Quarter on Bourbon Street. The five of us kept up the rent payment for years. Naked girls for beads was a great deal. In Colonial times, buying Long Island for beads may have been a better deal but not nearly as much fun. It was the month of May so having access to our apartment would be nothing. On top of being able to sit in a club listening to music all night, there was some fishing I was hearing about nearby.

This was about 1988. *A River Runs Through It* would not come out for about another four years. I mention that because, to me, that movie changed my sport profoundly. Before the movie, fly fishing was a quirky hobby filled with quirky people. The equipment was affordable and in some cases didn't yet exist. Often you would see something a guy made up to solve a problem. It would catch on and he could make a few bucks on it. After the movie, the sport got inundated with a yuppie subculture looking to fill the holes in their souls with something spiritual. Poor fuckers, they still don't get spirituality. They keep moving on to the next thing and pouring money into it and changing the landscape of whatever they touch. The baby boomers are like cattle that overgraze wherever they go. Before they got to fly fishing, the sport was a quirky small affair. We all sort of knew each other. It was an East and West thing. I was an East guy. I fished the Catskill Mountains quite a bit. Trout mostly were the game. Smallmouth bass were catching on. There was a smaller bunch of guys really into this saltwater stuff. You heard about it and your ears would perk up. The bonefish set was well-established but you really had to go far distances. This Gulf Coast stuff was closer.

A few months earlier we were playing Pensacola, Florida, and I happened to chat with a man who was telling me about catching redfish on a fly rod. He showed me some flies tied to look like small crabs. He swore if I caught a redfish on a fly I would forget about those "sissy" trout forever. He went on to tell me his fishing stories. I love fishing stories. They are mostly bullshit but it is necessary. Without the extras, it's like just slapping a steak on a stark white plate and saying "eat up!" I want the salad, the sorbet, the potatoes, gravy, asparagus, and crème brûlée. When he was through with his stories, the seeds were well planted. I started making calls. There was this guy in Thibodaux, Louisiana, named Dan. I called him and he assured me he knew how to catch redfish on a fly and I would "git 'em." Over the phone, he had a thick Cajun accent and a colorful manner. I figured at the very worst it would be entertaining. I booked Dan for the three days following the Mobile George Carlin show. I was pretty juiced up about it.

After the Carlin show on Saturday night I turned to my driver, Harry, who was also a lifelong friend, and said, "I am going to the Big Easy . . . you coming?" He acknowledged that three days was too short to go home. Yes, he was coming although he might just pass on the fishing part. I was fine with that. Flyfishermen are like bad drug peddlers. We want to share our wonderful obsession with friends but we soon learn that it is best to let it happen on its own. Having been in on a couple coerced fishing trips I can attest to uncomfortable angst. Besides, being left-handed makes you a bit self-conscious. With another guy in the boat you are always trying to throw your cast after he has already thrown his. If you don't fly fish it is like a lefty at the dinner table with a nine-foot arm. So being the only caster in the boat was something I loved.

On the road sleep came hard; that was always a bad part. Scheduling often called for grueling all-night drives with scant hours of sleep stolen from a day. With the day off we decided to sleep that night in a Marriott. The next morning we took the road less traveled. Most folks would take Highway 10 to New Orleans; we took Coastal Route 90. It runs along the Gulf. If you travel enough you learn certain things go with certain areas. Along the Gulf Shore from the Florida Panhandle well west of Louisiana there used to be oyster bars. Some are still there but not in the numbers and with the regional influence that used to be found there. The best ones were simply a counter you sat at outside. The very best were within sight and smell of the Gulf of Mexico. You would sit down and order a dozen shucked oysters, raw on the half shell. They would bring them out to you on ice or on a chilled plate. Any oyster aficionado will tell you that each locale had its own specific flavor. Some will even claim taste can vary from reef to reef. The oyster, though important, is only part of the event. The other thing these areas have is hot sauce. It is such a part of the culture here that loyalty to brands rivals the Red Sox or Yankees debate in baseball. Most places had Tabasco or Frank's but if you asked, "Do you have anything . . . else?"—a twinkle would develop in the eye of the person asked. "Well, we got this stuff . . ." they would say. It was *that* stuff I was always after. Most of it was very local and tasty. Occasionally you would be warned: "I dunno, it's really hot." The macho in you would think, how hot can it be? Dave's Insanity Sauce. You would think if they bothered to put "insanity" in the name, you should take heed. I am a victim of American marketing hype in the era of Madison Avenue's mastery so I expected less than insanity. *Fuck me!* One drop and I was on the ground rolling around like the idiot I was. Looking up with tears in my eyes, the guy said: "I told you it was hot." I am told it is still on the market. Try it, suffer, and think of me. The real point is that most of the time you came across all these local wonderful sauces. The art was taking a properly chilled oyster and adding a dab of the local hot sauce and sucking it in and enjoying it. After that, washing it down with ice-cold beer. The beer like the sauce was often varied. Each stand had their own way of approaching perfection. Some places added horseradish to the mix. It was usually the wild stock that required the wearing of goggles when it was grated. You would be tempted to order multiple dozens but you wouldn't. The fear was you would be too full for the next bar and miss out on the "*one*." This can make the trip from Mobile to New Orleans a really long journey. I have an Odysseus complex so really long journeys are at the core of my being. It was around nine o'clock Sunday night when we got into the French Quarter apartment.

Harry and I met in freshman year in high school. It was an all-boys Jesuit Catholic school. Most parents sent their sons there because it was felt that was exactly what they needed. In most cases it was exactly what they *didn't* need. At twelve years old it did not take very long for me to understand why the Catholic church excommunicated the Jesuits for three hundred years. However, it did allow you to make close lifelong friends. I don't see Harry as often as I like but in our hearts that friendship will always remain. We seem to drift in and out of each others lives over time. It is a shame that we drift less as we age. I still pop in on him from time to time. It works.

We got our stuff put up. I asked Harry if he was up for pounding the Quarter with me. I knew he would be. It was Sunday night so it was somewhat subdued but everything is relative. A subdued night in New Orleans is still something good. In most parts of the world it wouldn't be a wild night. The apartment was above some tourist trap souvenir shop. You came down a dirty staircase and the door opened up onto Bourbon Street. It was a good spot. It was easy to rent an apartment there if you were willing to pay rent year-round. This was in the middle of everything. You could sit in front of the door and listen to where you needed to be. Rather, where you needed to start. Music and laughter penetrated to air. We walked to the sound. I don't recall the place. In New Orleans you have the places that are legendary. Then you have the rest. The legends remain through it all. This was not one of those places. It was quaint with the jukebox shouting its music. There were people all around. There was a table with a bunch of pretty young ladies who where having a great time. I looked at Harry and he looked at me and we decided to take the bar stools very near the table. As we ordered drinks we listened in. I know it is not polite but . . . well, you know, young men on the prowl. I am just glad I can recall the prowl.

The girls were there for a bachelorette weekend. That was a mixed review. You had to figure at least one was unavailable. The music was getting to me. I love music. Almost all genres move me and given the right blend of music and atmosphere I can get going. I was liking what was pouring out of the jukebox so I figured I should like what should pour from the bottle. I ordered a couple shots of tequila for Harry and me. We were getting to it. We had the limes and the salt. All the while this little voice in my head kept telling me I needed to be in a car headed to Thibodaux at 4:30 a.m. It's funny how we can ignore that little voice if we want to.

She pushed her way up to the bar, partly knocking the shot I was attempting down the side of my face. She looked at what she had done and laughed. She was half drunk. She was beautiful. She had strawberry blond hair with a red cast to it. Her eyes were green, green, green—some would use a hokey simile "like emeralds" but her eyes were beyond that. She had this great smile and freckles across a turned-up nose. Life Savers were glued to her shirt and written in marker was "lick me." She said, "I am so sorry, can I buy you another one?" I said "Sure." I was always so smooth.

She told me her name was Allison and asked if she could sit next to me. We started talking and I was smitten. I was always a sucker for pretty little Irish girls. She was here from some place in Iowa and she was going to get married in a couple weeks. Her future husband-to-be went to Mexico to celebrate the end of his single life. Allison wanted the same consideration and took her bridesmaids for a weekend. I looked at Harry and like a couple of hunting dogs that had worked together for a long time, he had a pitcher of beer over at the table and was introducing himself to the rest of "the girls."

"You know, I can't drink this shot alone. Will you have one with me?" I asked. She obliged. Then another. I could start to feel the alcohol. The little voice said 4:30. I asked about the Life Savers on her shirt. She said I should try one. I leaned over and nibbled one off. I love that word nibble. It has such naughty overtones, just delicious like that particular Life Saver. Before I could tell what flavor it was one of the girls came off her chair at the table and was chiding Allison. After a bit of discourse, the fat girl sat back in her seat with her arms crossed and a frown.

"She looks too young to be your mom," I said.

"She's my fiancé's sister. I think she came to watch over me. Fuck her. This is my weekend."

I just smiled and ordered more shots. Still that voice persisted. A song came on the jukebox. Her eyes lit up. It was Robbie Robertson's "Somewhere Down the Crazy River." I was a big fan of The Band. They were a Canadian-American band. Being a man who grew up on the shores of Lake Ontario, Canadian radio was an influence. Also if you knew music history you knew The Band lived with Bob Dylan in his pink house in Saugerties, New York, on the east side of the Catskill Mountains. The Band's great album *Music from Big Pink* is what came out of that house. Some of Dylan's best tunes were written there, as well. I took a day in college and drove up to the house to see it. It wasn't much but you could feel the vibe. We went fishing near there and had a decent day. It was before cell phones and Internet and you had to fill your days doing stuff. Imagine that. Seeing Big Pink and doing a little fishing near there was a perfectly good way to kill a day. So coming fully around the barn I was a Robbie Robertson fan and my eyes must have lit up, as well. Allison asked me to please dance with her. Her request was simple enough. I had danced before. I didn't like it. Not that I was horrible—no one ever pointed and giggled—I just was never comfortable. Years later, I had a conversation with a good older friend. Somehow the conversation came around to women and fishing. Don acknowledged that there were women who fished. In fact if you ever saw Joan Wulff fly cast, it is amazing. She is better than any man I have ever seen. That is not the point—Don was saying that a lot of women go fishing with men. In his case his wife would go all the time. Once she was secure in their marriage, she stopped. He felt it was pretty common for women to use this in the course of courting an outdoorsman. The observation was without malice in Don's recounting because he said he did the same. That he would go dancing with her at first. That he quit about the same time he felt secure in their marriage. I laughed and recited a quote I had heard attributed to Voltaire: "If you can't dance you fuck a lot of waitresses." Don said there weren't enough waitresses so guys danced. It meant a lot to Allison to dance to that song. She pulled me off the stool and over to the smallish dance floor. We danced apart at first. There is a line in the song where the girl says, "Hang the rich!" And Allison was shouting that line with her arms over her head. She looked so beautiful and fun at the moment. I couldn't help myself; I flashed a big smile. She couldn't help herself; she pulled me to her and kissed me deeply and hot. Chemistry is a hell of a thing. There is that Beatles song "With a Little Help from my Friends" in which John Lennon asks, "Would you believe in love at first sight?" and then answers, "Yes, I'm certain that it happens all the time." It might happen all the time but this was the first time for me. To be honest, it was a very rare occurrence in my life. It may happen all the time—but like lightening, rarely striking the same spot twice. Enraptured in the embrace you can imagine how off guard I was when the fat girl shot between us like a linebacker shooting the gap off center. She broke into a tirade about how that was it and she was ending the night right there and then. Allison looked at me shaking her head. During the mayhem I looked at Harry and he winked. He knew what I wanted. Allison grabbed me. "Take me out of here," she said. Harry pulled the fat girl toward the bar and shouted, "I wanna buy the bar a round on me!" People flocked to the bar not wanting to miss the opportunity for free alcohol. By the time the fat girl pushed her way to the door Allison and I were gone.

I knew right where I wanted to take her. It was a place that oozed history. I was dragging her by the hand. We had to get out of sight of the fat girl. Finally we were in front of the Maison Bourbon. A place venerated by the ghost of blues-and-jazz greats. There is a sign that hangs over the front door: "Maison Bourbon dedicated to the Preservation of Jazz." From inside I heard a sweet sound. I started grinning like the Cheshire Cat. I took Allison in and knew she would be blown away. There was a good-looking young crooner at the keyboards. I was hoping Harry would be there. I had been coming there to see this guy. Harry Connick Jr. had been working the club hard and he was really starting to get noticed. It was so good. Did you ever wing it but all the pieces came together just right? This evening was like that. We danced and we kissed. She held her body close to mine. We both knew what was happening. We both knew how it would go. In the moment it didn't matter. The drinks continued to flow. We continued to dance and the chemistry continued to sizzle. Time, in its relentless arbitrary way, ticked on. She looked at me and said, "I have to go." I gave her half a smile and said, "I know."

I walked her to almost where I found her. It would be time to say goodbye. I held her and looked down into her face. Tears were streaming onto her cheeks. I told her I had fun. That I felt the same way she did. I promised I would always remember that night. She told me she wished we met at another time under different circumstances. That I stole her heart. How this just really messed things up. I kissed her and she squeezed me tight. I watched her walk toward where her friends were. We never exchanged numbers or addresses. She was going to be Mrs. Iowa Housewife. This was her selfish memory. The one she would look back on when times with Mr. Iowa Husband were less than good.

As for me? I can't really say what happened. I fell in love with a beautiful woman one night and that was that. Another guy might have tried to hang on and make something of it. I just felt it would be too complicated. I looked at my watch and it was well after 3:00 a.m.

I opened the door and Harry was sitting in a chair with a fifth of tequila in his hand. He had waited up for me. "So," he said sporting a big grin.

"So what?" I said.

I knew it could never be left at that. I gave him a brief accounting of the night. I knew I was never going to be able to sleep. It was already 4:00 a.m. I needed to get ready. I only had one big problem. I was in no shape to drive. Harry suggested I take an expensive cab ride (cheap in comparison to some of the possible consequences) and he would sleep his off. Then when he came around he would pack the stuff and drive to Thibodaux. Harry knew me and knew that I probably needed a little distance from this night. He said, "Besides I want a better version than the lame-ass crib note you just spewed at me." He handed me the tequila. I looked at him. "Hair of the dog!" he said, laughing: "You're going to need it!"

We stumbled to the cab and loaded it up. I somehow got to the place in Thibodaux around the time I needed to be there. How? I just don't recall. I probably managed to sleep.

I poured out of the cab. I was a fucking mess. I looked like hell, reeked of booze, was unshaven, and had on a dark pair of Ray Bans. I'm sure the Cajun guide was thinking, "Damn Yankee! This is gonna suck."

I paid the driver, grabbed my gear, and followed the guide. He threw my stuff in the back of his pickup. It was obvious he was not amused by my grand entrance. To be honest I wasn't amused very much myself. My brain had already started to swell, putting pressure against my cranium causing increasing discomfort. In other words, the mother of all hangovers was starting. I had thoughts of bailing, but my truck and Harry were in New Orleans. If there was ever starting off on the wrong foot, this was it. There were a few times in my life I had filled in as a last-minute replacement for a guide at a friend's fishing lodge and over the years I have gotten to be close friends with a few licensed guides. The one thing that runs through the brotherhood of guides everywhere is the distain for a bullshit client. It is expected that as a client there are minimums of competency that should be brought to the trip. On a fishing trip, the expectations are low. As low as they are, I was really screwing the pooch.

"Late night?" he asked.

"Uh-huh," I whispered.

His next question was, "Is this how you boys go fishing in New York?" It was one of those questions when so much more just happened. You know for sure he's pissed. He is also letting you know that he cannot believe you showed up for a trip like this. That perhaps you have no regard for him. Finally, he has some deep-seated issues with the result of the Civil War. I felt like Quasimodo was ringing the bell from Notre Dame right in my head. I looked at him through the pounding trying to formulate the correct answer.

"It is," I said. There seemed to be a long silence. It lasted all the way to the dock. At the dock we started to move my gear to the boat. Silence still hung in the air. We were stringing up my rod and a screwed up look came over his face. He was looking all over my rod for anything to tell him what it was. It was a rod I had put together a couple of winters before. It was a G. Loomis nine-foot, 8-weight blank on which I wrapped gunmetal blue guides with red thread wraps and black stripes. My hands are large so I put on a thick cigar grip with Spanish cork. The reel seat was burled maple with a gunmetal blue cap. In the arrogance of my youth, I painted where the manufacture's logo usually goes "Jerry's Killer." What it really ended up being was a sturdy 8-weight with a nice medium to fast action. I have taken that rod to many places and caught scores of fish on it. I still have her. Unlike many of today's makers, Jerry's rods never came with a replacement guarantee. I finally retired her before I broke her. Flyfishermen can get attached to their stuff. That is why, when they pass away, their kids ultimately say, "Look at all this shit! What are we going to do with it? I think we are going to need a dumpster." If by some chance my disembodied spirit hears that I hope I get to haunt my children.

Finally, Dan the angry Cajun guide asked me: "What the hell is this?"

I said, "It's Jerry's Killer." I knew I was being a smart ass but at this point this is where we were.

"I see," he said. "It feels kind of light. Maybe today Jerry's Killer gets killed?"

"So you think you might find a fish like that?" I was baiting him a bit.

"I GAR-ON-TEE IT!" he answered.

In a way, it was a good moment. With that thick Cajun accent weaving through my hangover, all the pride and irritation—the virtual *gar-on-tee* that there would be fish—loosened things up a bit. He looked at the Abel reel and started to loosen up a bit more. It was a well-matched outfit. He must have at least figured that I might be able to live up to his promise.

Penance can be paid in so many ways. This day mine would be paid in the boat ride to where we were going to fish. The boat was a tidy center-console affair. It had ample horsepower to navigate almost all the conditions encountered in the Gulf.

I noticed Dan was taking the waves at such an angle as to maximize the chop in the boat. I had the mother of all hangovers and he wanted to punish me. There was really only one thing to do. Discreetly I poured several shots of tequila into my coffee. I will tell you that this is not a culinary delight. It did help. Eventually we pulled onto the flats. The boat was rigged with a high platform from which the guide would pole the boat. The platform was at the rear of the boat and the fisherman was at the front. Stern and bow for you boat people.

I had opened a book of flies looking for something to tie on. Dan looked at my hands with great interest. If I have a weakness it is flies. I have tried to tie them. I can sit with an instruction book open in front of me and tie them. They ultimately come out looking like the photo. I know of guys who just get the biggest kick out of catching a fish on a rod they built with a fly they tied. I really get that. In fact I have even done it, once. In the end my flies come out like a paint-by-number painting. There are artists who can tie a thing of beauty. When you put one of their flies next to mine it just feels different. If it was only looks that would be superficial. The real master's flies fish differently too.

Every time I go on a trip I try to find the best flies. I have flies from some of the greatest tiers. I even have a signed fly book from Lee Wulff. I won't fish those, but all the others have been in the water.

I picked a fly from the book. The guide looked with a sideways glance. I could tell he wasn't sure. He was smart enough to stay quiet. It was maybe a new fly, or just vaguely familiar. I never had seen any before this batch came in the mail. While I was in Florida I had done a little running around. Seems there was this fly-fishing guide who had come up with a fly that was really slamming redfish. Eventually, I managed to get his name and phone number. The guide was and still is Jon B. Cave. I called him up. I told him I wanted to buy some of his Cave's Wobblers. If you have never seen one, it's really a spoon fly. Cave's Wobblers fish so well that you will never twist a line. Jon was happy to field my call. We ended up talking for a long time. It is that way among fishermen. We need to share our tales. He said he was curious how they would work in Louisiana. I was going to find out. I tied on a little copper-colored Wobbler. It looked good.

On this trip, we were sight-fishing. The guide, who was high upon his platform, would spot fish and tell me where to cast. That morning, I was casting anyway. With the hangover and the sun I needed to get a rhythm. I started casting and casting. You can get into a zone that way. Sort of like auto pilot. Then your mind just starts to go. It can be real good. I started to recall the night before. Under my breath I was humming the Robbie Robertson song.

> *Yeah I can see it now*
> *The distant red neon shivered in the heat*
> *I was feeling like a stranger in a strange land*
> *You know where people play games with the*
> *night*
> *God, it was too hot to sleep . . .*
> *Catch the blue train*
> *to places never seen before.*
> *Look for me*
> *Somewhere down the crazy river*
> *somewhere down the crazy river*
> *Catch the blue train . . .*

That tune was stuck in my head. I was wondering about Allison. "Two o'clock, two o'clock!" Dan roared. Instinctively my cast rolled out to two o'clock. The Wobbler worked its magic. "Eleven . . . eleven o'clock!" Slam—another redfish was pulling line. This one was better than the first. I was in the zone. The guide kept bird-dogging me directions and my casts were on. By midmorning I had the bottle out in the open and was starting to feel better. The day was getting hot. I had that sweat where the alcohol comes through your pores. At first it hurts but then it's detoxifying. There wasn't the usual banter between guide and client. It didn't matter because we fell into a groove. There was a rhythm now between him and I. We were kicking the shit out of it. We boated more than thirty redfish before noon. I noticed the guide's scowl had faded quite a bit. It was mid-afternoon and the pace had never let up. New flies were tied on as the old ones gave out. I was holding up my end, hangover and all. The tune just kept rolling around in my head. I was just doing what I could to keep in the zone.

During mid-afternoon, the cadence was broken. Dan's voice came forth in a harsh whisper. "Giant red at one! Giant red at one!" I could see the fish. There is something so primal when we get onto giant quarry. It can be a huge buck, a twenty-inch brook trout, or a three-foot-plus redfish and the sight of them makes the adrenal glands open wide. Here I was with my body half inebriated and half hungover surging with adrenaline anticipating a shot at a giant. Some guys say it doesn't affect them but it has to. It is better in fishing in so far as if you choke all that happens is nothing. Nothing to the fish. Most fisherman carry those moments for a lifetime. I can still close my eyes and see a thirty-pound-plus northern pike pull off my fly and send back a pigtailed leader. It happened more than twenty years ago and I test my knots frequently since.

It is the kind of situation you get one shot at. The fish are cruising and they get by you quickly. This fish was really large so it was easy to see. It was a cast I had been making all day. I could build this up to a big moment where the cavalry comes charging in . . . but fly fishing is not like that. It is far more subtle. I still had the zone going but the rhythm was broken a bit. Like when the opposing coach calls a time-out to ice the kicker. The cast was there, the fish took, the fight was on. It took a brief moment to get into the backing. I had to slow down the fish. I cupped the Abel reel's spool with as much tension as I dared. My homemade rod had the full parabolic arc. I was thinking about Dan's words "Killing Jerry's Killer." Several times I could see the knot on the reel's arbor (meaning the end of the line had literally been reached). I was able to turn the fish. All the while Dan kept the boat moving, poling hard toward the fish. Here we were again in perfect simpatico. It took some time but the redfish was at the side of the boat. We were both exhilarated. Dan quickly weighed her and revived her. Redfish are very good table fare. We did not even consider keeping her or any of the other fish. The problem was how good they were to eat. A restaurant in New Orleans started a literal feeding frenzy with its extraordinary dish— Blackened Redfish. The demand was insatiable. Redfish stocks were decimated. With that story as the backdrop, this hundred-fish day was unlikely. Unlikely and amazing. The girl weighed more than thirty-eight pounds.

After she was released, I sat on the seat and Dan sat next to me. He was tired; so was I. It was the first break we took all day. I took a pull from the tequila bottle and handed it to him. He took a long pull. I remember looking at him and thinking how tough he looked for an old guy. I was in my late twenties; he was probably fifty. As I write this I am fifty. With the years, the story has a different feel. Over time my part has become more brash and his more wise. Enlightenment of some sort. We sat and started talking. I told him about the previous evening. He started to laugh. He had a similar story about a woman in college but the barrier was religion. He was a Baptist and she was a Presbyterian. On some level he could relate to a dead-end love. We drank the rest of the bottle together. It was a picturesque evening and we soaked it in. He asked me about the flies and I told him about Jon Cave. It turns out we had caught enough fish that day.

The trip in was pleasant. As we pulled up to the dock I was thinking about the day. It started out with as much anger and angst as it could have. Now here we were coming in lifted and happy. With a genuine respect and affection toward each other. Therein lies the power of fishing. It has restorative qualities. It can calm all sorts of troubled waters. Really it is the power of nature. If we can just listen to her voice it can heal. If there is a God, and I say that because I am no theologian, one of His greatest gifts is allowing us to hear the cadences of the natural world we are part of. If there is no God, what an incredible accident.

Harry was waiting for me at the dock. He met Dan and after hearing about the day's fishing he decided to come out the next couple of days. Of course they would not rival the first one. It was good. The three of us seemed to get along great. So good in fact that Dan invited Harry and me to a boil. In the south—in Bayou Country, to be exact—a boil is like a New England clam bake. It is only like it in that you cook a lot of good food outdoors and the guest of honor has two claws. The boil is about lots of boiled crawfish, otherwise known as crawdads or mudbugs. Like anything else in Cajun cooking, it's all about the spices. It is also about the beer. What else? Corn on the cob, small potatoes of color (red, yellow, purple), lots of garlic, onions (*ohnyons*), lemons, Andouille sausage, head-on shrimp, asparagus, and enough butter to excite your cardiologist. Everyone has this or that added or exchanged but it is a wonderful party. The best ones have a Zydeco band blaring in the background. I had been to boils but this one was different. The ones I had been to were for a church or some other community event. This was for an individual's eightieth birthday.

It had that special inside feeling. I got slapped on the back a lot and told I was okay for a "Yankee." I would say, "Hell, I'm an Orioles fan!"

After a while and a bunch of beers, things started to thin out. There is always that moment when it's time to say goodbye. Sometimes it's harder than others. Things happened on this trip. Unexpected things happened. I always like it when my life story has a plot twist. I was walking toward Dan the guide and he was anticipating what was coming. "Ah think we got time for one more," he said, "there's thet place just pass theh levy." Pointing over a-ways, we followed the street along the levy. Eventually the local watering hole came into view. It had two neon Budweiser signs in each window on either side of the open door. It was a warm late-May evening. The jukebox was blaring. A melody came wafting from the open maw of the bar. Wouldn't you know it:

> *Yeah I can see it now*
> *The distant red neon shivered in the heat*
> *I was feeling like a stranger in a strange land*
> *you know where people play games with the night*
> *God, It was too hot to sleep . . .*
> *I followed the sound of a jukebox coming from a levee*
> *All of a sudden I could hear somebody whistling*
> *from right behind me*
> *I turned around and she said*
> *"Why do you always end up down at Nick's Café?"*
> *I said "I don't know, the wind just kind of*
> *pushed me this way."*
> *She said "Hang the rich"*
>
> *Catch the blue train*
> *To places never been before.*

Look for me.
Somewhere down the crazy river
(somewhere down the crazy river).

Take a picture of this
The fields are empty, abandoned '59 Chevy
Laying in the backseat listening to Little Willie John
Yeah, that's when time stood still
You know, I think I am gonna go down to Madam X
And let her read my mind
She said "that voodoo stuff don't do nothing for me."

I'm a man with a clear destination
I'm a man with a broad imagination
You fog the mind, you stir the soul
I can't find, no control

Catch the blue train
To places never been before
Look for me
Somewhere down the crazy river
(somewhere down the crazy river)
Catch the blue train
All the way to Kokomo
You can find me
Somewhere down the crazy river
(somewhere down the crazy river)

Wait, did you hear that?
Oh, this is sure stirring up some ghost for me
She said, "There's one thing you have got to learn
Is not to be afraid of it"
I said "No, I like it, I like it it's good."

She said, "You like it now
But you'll learn to love it later."

I been spellbound falling in trances
I been spellbound falling in trances
You give me shivers, chills and fever
You give me shivers
You give me shivers
I been spellbound, I been spellbound
I been spellbound somewhere down the crazy river
somewhere down the crazy river.

This kind of blew my mind. We all smiled. All weekend I was talking about how I was on this Blue Train. This crazy zigzag adventure. The lasting thing to come away from this weekend was that phrase. When we would contemplate a crazy last-minute or just logistically challenged trip we would call it Catching the Blue Train. For years it has been so. Many of the passengers are long gone. Most don't even know where the name came from. Human memory is so fascinating. As animals we remember things as a preservation mechanism. As humans we remember for so many other reasons. Things can trigger a memory buried deeply. I had a brief stint where I was smoking a pipe. I was outside where some people were. A woman came up to me with tears in her eyes. She asked, "Is that Borkum Riff Cherry Tobacco?" It was. She apologized and said her father used to smoke that around Christmas.

Sound is another big trigger. Sometimes when that song comes on the radio I wonder what happened to Allison. If she remembers like I do. I wonder about fishing redfish in Louisiana. I always wanted to go back but never did. Now that I am a bit older I think having the perspective helps. Redfish recovery has been a real fisheries-management success story. I think I will go back and catch some redfish on a fly. I might just have one blackened and eat it. I have been catching the Blue Train for more than twenty-five years. I think you are bound to backtrack.

Chapter 15:
The Dream

"Dreams are true while they last, and do
we not live in dreams?"

—*Alfred Lord Tennyson*

Author's Note: In examining what dreams meant to older
cultures—I use the term *older* instead of *primitive*—I have
concluded that their power is in the vision.

I wake up from sleep. I am in a room. It is my room. I feel good
and well-rested. I sit up on my bed. It is not any bed I recognize. It
is narrow and simple. I look around the room. There are windows
but they have no glass. They just open to the other side. The door
is the same. It is an opening to the outside. The walls look and
feel like plaster. They are off-white, almost gray. There is nothing
on them. There are no furnishings at all. At the foot of my bed
are old friends. There is Bal, a golden retriever that I owned and
loved. There are also two Persian cats, Ginger and Leroy. They
are waiting for me. As I swing my feet to the floor I can feel the
smooth surface. My old friends approach and I am happy to see

them again. I feel a lump in my throat. I put out my hand to see if they are real. I spend much time with them. It is all there right down to the texture of their fur.

I get up and walk to the door. I peer outside. I can see that this is a village of sorts. The arrangement has a center with a fire pit and well-worn seating around it. I look to the right and notice a plain oak bench about four feet long. It is placed against my hut. Next to it are four fly rods. They are arranged neatly and separated by pegs. Under my bench is my green canvas fly-fishing bag.

I move toward the bench and sit on it. I reach under the seat to pull my bag out. I look inside and see beautiful leather fly books. They are full of finely tied flies. I looked to my right and see the rods and reels. Some I recognize—actually, two I recognize and two I don't. I recognize my Baginski 4-weight and my Leonard 5-weight. The reels attached to them are Peerless and they are just pristine. The other two rods are made of bamboo, as well. There are no markings to identify these rods. As I lift them and wave them I am comfortable calling them the 3-weight and 6-weight. My old friends have found me again and are at my feet.

I sit there for some time. I keep looking at the rest of the village. There seems to be no activity. The air is sweet and cool. The sky is cornflower blue with the occasional high cirrus cloud. The temperature is very comfortable. I look at my feet and they are bare. The earth around my bench is soft and dry, perhaps a bit dusty. I look up and see a figure walking toward me. It is vague and yet familiar. As it gets closer I recognize the man. He is my grandfather. I cannot talk; my eyes are welling up. He asks me if I am going fishing today. I look at him. His demeanor is casual and warm. I cannot find my voice; I just nod my head. He tells me "good" and then says he will see me after.

I watch as he moves to another hut. I stand and grab the 4-weight and my bag. I begin to walk toward the back of my hut.

I notice I am on the edge of my area. The farthest from the fire pit. Ahead is a field of goldenrod. It is about knee height.

I begin to walk into the field and my friends follow. They seem to be enjoying that we are moving. Time seems to go by but I cannot tell how much. The sun seems to move. After some time I can see a stream come into focus.

As I get to the water's edge, the stream is about twenty or thirty yards wide. I watch the water. After a while, I notice that a hatch is starting. Eventually I do notice rises and that it is a sparse green-drake hatch. I remember seeing some size 8s in one of the boxes. I tie one on and test the knot.

I wade into the stream just below a riffle. There is a nice small pool behind a rock. It looks just perfect.

I cast and the fly floats to the back of the pool. Very quickly a trout rolls on the fly. I make several more casts. A trout rises and then turns away. I think they are brown trout. I will need to catch one to see. I keep casting but nothing is taking. I snap off my fly and tie on something smaller. After a couple of poor casts, I finally put the fly delicately on the water. I mend the line ever so slightly and the fish takes. I set the hook and the rod bends nicely toward the water. The dog and the two cats stand and move to the water's edge. In a short while, I work the fish to the side of the stream. It is a very pretty eighteen-inch brown trout. I admire it and set it back.

I wade in and begin to fish again. I notice how good the water feels on my legs. I fish for a while. I am noticing that the sun is getting low in the sky. I do not catch another fish but I enjoy the time. I call to my friends and we began to walk back to my village.

It was definitely evening as the sun was lower and shadows were getting longer. I could see my hut now. I walked to it. I put my rod up and sat on my bench. I noticed my jeans were almost dry. At my feet were my friends. I motioned for them to come closer. The cats jumped up next to me and my dog was in front. I enjoyed petting them again. It was an old familiar feeling I was glad to have. I was not paying attention when a voice broke through.

"Are you coming, Jerry?"

I looked up and saw a young boy. "Who are you?" I asked.

"I am Joseph, I am an ancestor." I could not speak again. "Are you coming to the fire tonight?"

I said "yes." The boy turned and walked toward the center of the area, to the place where the fire was being prepared. There were old men stacking wood. I could just see a bit of it from my bench. The sun was behind my hut. It was starting to set. The sky was awash with the hues of red and orange and purple. It was a stunning sunset. I watched it. The colors faded and darkness crept in. Behind me I could pick up a flicker here and there from the great fire. It radiated an orange glow outward from its center. I was waiting for time to pass. I had some nervousness about leaving.

I arose from my bench. I walked toward the fire light. I could see the fire had people all around it. I could see faces illuminated in the glow. I was too far away to be able to recognize any. I moved closer. I could see an open seat near the back on the side I was standing. I thought I could discreetly move toward that seat and take it without bringing notice.

I slipped into the seat. It was next to a woman with a shawl around her shoulders. I just wanted to settle in without drawing attention. I kept my head down and listened. There was a man speaking. I noticed he was telling a story. It was about how he had to make cheese in an effort to raise the money for a dowry. There were times when everyone laughed. I was too apprehensive to laugh. The woman next to me put her hand upon mine and patted it reassuringly. I spent some time listening. As one story would end, someone else would move to the teller's spot and begin. I would not look up. I was more comfortable holding Ginger and listening with my head bent forward.

The voices ceased and people moved away. I took the opportunity to move briskly to my hut. I moved to the bed. It was dark but there were ribbons of moonlight seeping into the room through the windows. I sat in the middle and my old friends came into the hut and settled around the bed. At the foot of the bed was a thin white cotton blanket. I was neither cold nor warm. The thought of the blanket covering me brought comfort. As I lay with the blanket over me I could feel a wave of relaxation come over me. I was falling asleep.

My eyes opened and I looked at the smooth plaster ceiling. I was in my hut, still. I sat up in the bed and my old friends came to me. I recall enjoying the familiar texture of their coats. I felt good.

As I swung my feet to the floor, I could not recall the aches I earned over a life. My body felt whole and strong and clear and clean. I wanted to see myself but the room had nothing more than the bed and its complements. The walls and floor were smooth and without scuffs or scrapes. It was clearly my place. It was for sleeping. Nothing else.

I rose and walked out the door and my friends followed. I was pleased that they just knew to be with me. I found my bench as I had left it. My fly bag was next to me. My cats were on the bench with me and Bal was at my feet. The bench faced east. The sun had just come up and its yellow gold rays were making me squint.

I sat there enjoying the company. Leroy purred as loud as I ever remembered. I was in no hurry to do anything. It felt good to sit on my bench. Like the morning before, a figure was walking toward me. This morning I recognized it to be my grandfather. I just looked in that direction. My mouth was dry and I could not find words. As he came close, he smiled at me.

Will you fish today? I nodded my head yes. He told me I would have a guest. He put his hand on my shoulder.

"You must get going, Leonid will be waiting. Yesterday you went to the west. Today you must go to the north. He will probably be there before you."

In his hand, I felt comfort. Words just would not come. Even before, he was a formidable figure. Now he had no stoop and his step was sharp. It made his presence even more commanding. He patted me on the back as if to get me going. I reached for the fly outfit I used the day before.

He told me: "No. Not that. Take the 6-weight and some bass poppers." I grabbed the 6-weight and my bag. He was already moving on to the same direction he went yesterday.

I walked north. I was not sure who Leonid was but he was fishing with me today. My friends followed as I walked. I looked behind and my hut was a tiny dot toward the horizon. The sun was higher but still low enough to tell me it was before midmorning. In a while longer a river came into view. In a little more time the outline of a big man was there. I moved closer and could see a large smile with heavy jowls on either side. There was an Eastern European nose with twinkling eyes on each side and above those were very bushy eyebrows. In fact the eyebrows were prominent. There was something very familiar to his face.

He said: "The morning is nearly gone. You Americans are always tardy. I am Leonid Brezhnev."

I was having recall. Here was the head of the Communist Party and the Soviet Union and we were to fish together. He asked me if it was okay if he fished my river with me this day. I told him that I was pleasured to be fishing with him.

We were at a great bend in a midsize river. There was a gravel bar where the current deposited the gravel. You could wade the bar for a bit. It dropped sharply just past the edge of the bar. It was hard to tell how deep. You could see the bottom but it would blur as the current pushed. I saw the man push out some distance on the bar and start to throw a popper to the far bank over the deep water. I pulled out my fly book with the poppers. I tied on a red-and-white Umpqua bass popper. It had a solid and thick black stripe dividing the red from the white. Its tail was tied with red, white, and black dyed feathers. The finishing touches were the big eyes painted on each side. I always liked Umpqua bass poppers. It felt familiar and right here.

I sidled along that gravel bar and stopped about ten feet from Leonid. I asked him about his comment that this was my river.

He said, "This is your place. All the spots around here are yours. No one can fish them but you and with you."

"How is it you and I are here together?"

"Your ancestors thought you might like some company today. I have wanted to fish here for a very long time. Actually, lots of people want to fish your places with you. It is told that they are special. Full of big and willing fish. Some say that when you catch a fish in your life it eventually comes to your places."

At that point a nice smallmouth bass hit my popper, hard. I set up on the fish and it pulled hard. My reel screamed as line came off. The fish tail walked across the water. In a few more minutes it spit my popper. We looked at each other and smiled. All through the morning we chatted and fished. The conversation went from one thing to the other. At one point he, half kidding, made a comment about a capitalist trying to fish.

"It is better than a bunch of Communists trying to share a poorly made rod." I went on to say: "I am really a constitutionalist and capitalism was its necessary byproduct."

"It is that corruption of business bleeding into the political system that makes it so oppressive."

I looked at him sideways and started to laugh. He smiled and said, "Well that's the way it's supposed to work!" Then he asked if I was a Democrat or Republican.

I said, "Neither. The Democrats think I am too stupid to take care of myself. That the government must protect me from myself. In my need they create and administer programs I don't want and eventually can't afford. The Republicans think everyone is dishonest and they must protect me from everyone else. In the process of keeping me free, they exploit and diminish my freedoms. The truth is I just want to be left alone. I guess that makes me a Libertarian. Just give me my democratic republic and some good fishing."

I did not get to finish my rant when my popper got smacked again. These bass fought hard. I landed a dandy fish. It was an easy three pounds. I set her back. The afternoon went that way. We would go from one subject to another. He talked about his days in Land Management when he was young. How it was there he first learned to love fishing. I kept landing nice fish with regularity. Finally Leonid asked me if I had another red and white popper. I told him I did but I would need a buck. He frowned and said, "There is no money here."

It was okay, as I already had the popper out and handed it to him. When he realized I was playing he called me a bourgeois American. I smiled and called him a self-righteous Commie.

He tied on the new popper. I took a moment to watch. Leonid placed a nice cast right up against the high bank on the far side of the river. He began to twitch the popper ever so slightly. I watched with anticipation. Like a pregnant pause, the popper sat on the water. Then a large bronzeback came out of the water and engulfed the fly.

Brezhnev's eyes lit up as he fought the large fish. In time he had what appeared to be a five-pound smallmouth by the jaw. He looked up and smiled a large grin.

"This is the biggest bass I have ever caught." Gently and with purpose, he returned the giant.

We fished and talked until the sun started to get low. We waded off the gravel bar. He went to hand me my popper and I told him he could keep it. He shook his head. "No, I cannot.

It is yours and it must stay with you. I thank you for letting me fish here with you. All days here are good. Some are so good they stand out. I will remember that fish. I will remember you."

We shook hands and recalled some of the finer points of the day. I began to walk south with my friends following. I began recounting the day in my head. I had fished with Leonid Brezhnev. We chatted all day. Our views were completely opposite but I enjoyed the gentle debate. There was no malice or aggressive passion. Just two men genuinely enjoying stimulating conversation. Knowing for this day to be as perfect as it was each man had to hold up his end of the day. The whole thing was so good. Its best moment was watching him land the big bass. It was a flawless day. It was heaven.

I was almost back to my hut. I kept playing the day over in my head. It was a pleasant breeze blowing through my hair. I was at my bench and I put up my rod and bag. I sat at my bench and looked toward the fire pit. I could see the old men stacking up the wood for tonight's fire. It would be time soon. As I glanced to my left I could see an older woman coming toward me. I stood up. As she neared I recognized her. "Nana," I whispered.

"Oh Honey," she said as she embraced me. I put my head on her shoulder. I grabbed her tight. I understood so little here. She was a comfort.

"I came to see you. I heard you were here so I came."

"Oh Nana, I was here yesterday too. I did not see you."

"Honey, this is not my fire. Men have to sit at the fire of their line. Woman can sit at their fire or choose to sit at the fire of one of their children. I can sit with you at your fire tonight. If you want me to." She smiled.

"I would love that," I said. "I know only grandfather here. Everyone else is a stranger."

"They are your people. This is your fire. In time you will know them and all the stories. In time you will be closer to the fire than the newest. I don't know how it is you are here. It is not your time. You will have to go back. I don't understand it. No one gets to see here before. I have never seen this, but you have to go back."

I looked at her. I was just here. I told her I had no answers. She reassured me that things were in accordance to a plan. That for whatever reason I was here and it would work out. She went to the fire with me. Time after time pointing out people in the circle explaining who they were. How the connection came down to me. It made the stories they told better. It made them more a part of me. I think that was the idea. It was the history and nuance of my clan. All the while she hung onto my arm. The first night I sat low and with apprehension. This night I sat high with anticipation. As each teller would take the spot my grandmother would frame it with some pertinent background.

Time eventually passed until the embers went low and hot. My ancestors started to file away from the fireplace. I stood and looked at my Nana. She stood and cupped my face in her hands and kissed it. It had been done before. It was familiar and missed all at once. She told me she loved me and had to return to her place. I stood my ground as she walked away. I just watched and felt it all. Her words of the evening rang around my mind's eye.

My friends and I walked toward my hut. We crossed the threshold and I stood before my bed. I sat on the bed for a long time petting my furry friends. I just wanted to make the day stretch a little longer. I could feel sleep coming to me. It was an easy feeling. Like adding warm water to a bath. It gradually spread over me. I lay fully down and pulled the thin white blanket up to my chin. I woke in the morning. Tears were flooding my eyes. I made no noise other than breathing through my mouth. I was in my bedroom. My real bedroom. I could hear a car speeding way too fast down my road. I swung my feet to the floor. There I stayed with my head in my hands. The vision of the dream fresh in my head. Vivid in the recall. Every detail firmly in my memory. I stayed there for some time, mind fully blown.

I am sure there are those who would be willing to help me interpret my dream. Freud wrote a volume, *The Interpretation of Dreams*. My favorite quote is, "The Dream is the fulfillment of a Wish." I knew I wanted to be careful. In my soul I did not want to dismantle this dream. I liked my vision of heaven. Like all faith-based notions, scrutiny can screw them up. It would come to pass that months after this dream I would be diagnosed with Non-Hodgkin's lymphoma. In my battle there were hard days when the outcome was uncertain. During those days I often found comfort in my dream. I know that somewhere it is significant that I fish. It is here where I like the Alfred Lord Tennyson quote on dreams the best: "Dreams are true while they last, and do we not live in dreams?"

I hope we all get to live in our dreams.